Five Ideas That Change the World

Books by Barbara Ward

The West at Bay
Policy for the West
Faith and Freedom
The Interplay of East and West
Five Ideas That Change the World
India and the West
The Rich Nations and the Poor Nations
Nationalism and Ideology
Spaceship Earth
The Lopsided World
Only One Earth (with René Dubos)
The Home of Man
Progress for a Small Planet

BARBARA WARD

Five Ideas That Change the World

GREENWOOD PRESS, PUBLISHERS
WESTPORT, CONNECTICUT

Library of Congress Cataloging in Publication Data

Ward, Barbara, 1914–
  Five ideas that change the world.

    Reprint. Originally published: New York : W.W. Norton,
c1959.
    1. Nationalism. 2. Industrialization. 3. Colonies.
4. Communism. 5. Internationalism. I. Title. II. Title:
5 ideas that change the world.
JC311.J24 1984   320.5   84-6721
ISBN 0-313-24525-8 (lib. bdg.)

Reprinted in 1984 by Greenwood Press
A division of Congressional Information Service, Inc.
88 Post Road West, Westport, Connecticut 06881

Printed in the United States of America

10 9 8 7 6 5 4 3 2 1

Contents

Foreword

by The Prime Minister of Ghana

AT THE beginning of the 1957 academic year I suggested to the Principal of the University of Ghana that my good friend Lady Jackson, known to the world as Barbara Ward, might accept an invitation to give a series of public lectures at the University College on world affairs, a subject which seemed peculiarly fitting in the year of Ghana's attainment of independent nationhood. This book is the outcome.

So striking were the lectures themselves and so marked was the impact upon the audience, which became greater in numbers at each successive lecture, that I conceived the idea, supported by my colleagues in the Cabinet, of making available to the University College a yearly sum of money to found an annual series of lectures, of which this should be the first, to be called the "Aggrey-Fraser-Guggisberg Lectures" to commemorate the great work of these three men in the educational advance of the Gold Coast, now Ghana: A. G. Fraser, the founder and inspirer of the great traditions of Achimota School and its first Principal; J. E. K. Aggrey, his able, loyal and devoted first lieutenant, whose saying "only the best is good enough for Africa" has been a watchword of the school; and Sir Gordon Guggisberg, Governor of the Gold Coast from 1919 to 1927, who gave constant and enthusiastic support to their efforts. Without them, Ghana could not now lay claim to be as advanced in the educational field as any territory on the African continent.

It is so often said that an understanding of the present relies upon an understanding of the past; in the present age the truth of this is perhaps less patent than formerly. Never before has the world been so divided by conflicting ideologies, never has so much depended upon the finding, not, perhaps, of a reconciliation of the ideologies, but of a means of coexistence. The very continuation of the human race would seem to hang upon a solution of this problem.

Barbara Ward does not make the mistake common to many economists and political theorists of attempting to interpret the present, still less to prophesy the future, in terms solely of the past. Though in each of her lectures she traces for each of her fields the development of political thought from the earliest times, the great importance of the series lies in her analysis of the present and her synthesis of the components into a broad picture which explains while it informs.

She has a special message to the small, uncommitted countries: that they, free from the shackles of conflicting political ideologies, may play an important part in holding the ring for the main contestants, to prevent that loss of control which could mean the end of humanity. She quotes the African proverb, "When the bull elephants fight, the grass is trampled down" and pleads with the small and uncommitted nations to make their voices heard constructively while there is still time, for in this age of the ultimate weapon the bull elephants would disappear with the grass.

Through all these lectures runs a single thread, the inevitability of the freedom of man, even if that freedom is liberty for self-destruction. All history has shown that domination of man by man must in the end bring revolt, passive or active, when the right of the individual or the group triumphs over suppression. I said earlier that the past may no longer be a certain guide to the future; let us hope that in this one respect history will be the signpost, and that intolerance and exploitation and inhumanity of man to man may some day vanish from the earth.

Government House   KWAME NKRUMAH
Osu
Ghana

Five Ideas That Change the World

Chapter One

Nationalism

IN APPROACHING the
problems of our modern world we should, I think, try
to begin where the real center of power lies. I hardly
need to insist that underlying most issues in national
and international relations is the problem of power:
power in the simplest sense of men being able ultimately
to make other people do what they want. In our world,
this final power is exercised by the state: under a despotic government by force, under a democratic government largely by consent; but in the last analysis any kind
of government rests on its ability to impose its policies
and to achieve its will. This is the absolute sovereignty

exercised by the state alone.

The state is thus the nodal point of all our problems. Since we are concerned with world affairs, the aspect of the state which we have to study is largely its relations with other states. This is the field in which lie the tensions, the possibilities, the whole vista of international politics. But it might be as well to begin by looking at the state itself in isolation. We imagine we know what we mean when we talk of the state; yet it is a concept that has changed out of all recognition over the centuries. What we think about it today is not at all what our ancestors thought of it. Our own approach is obvious in such phrases as "the nation-state" or the "United Nations Organization." For us, "nation" and "state" seem interchangeable. But this is, in fact, quite a new concept. If we had been discussing the matter in the sixteenth century, we should not have mentioned the word "nation-state." Certainly we should have talked about "the state," but we should have been referring only to the center of political authority and not trying to define it. The power itself might be exercised by a dynasty, or by a conqueror, or a free city, or the Pope himself. No one would have thought automatically of the state being synonymous with the nation.

No, this master-institution of our modern international system has come into being only in the last three hundred years, and it is a perfectly modern idea that there is an essential link between nationalism and the state or that the sense of being a national group entails the right to achieve statehood.

How, then, has it arisen? Some of its roots, for all its modernity, are very old indeed. They go back to what was for perhaps a hundred thousand years the basic social institution of mankind, the tribe. This system, which is still a living reality only in Africa and in parts of Asia, was once universal. All our societies have in some measure developed from the original tribal pattern and it undoubtedly foreshadows some of the characteristics of our latter-day full-blooded nationalism. The first and strongest sense was that of kinship, of having closer connections with one group of men than with any others, the sense of being under a single authority. This unity of organization was reinforced by common traditions and customs, by legends and myths, and—a point of the utmost significance—by a common language. In New Guinea today the language changes virtually from village to village as you move from one kinship group to the next.

There is also the other side of the coin of union and of cohesion. This is the sense of *not* having close links with others and the consciousness of their being strangers, outside the group. From strangers to enemies is a short step, especially when their efforts, desires, and drives may, in fact, impede the activities of your own tribe. The earliest legends record not only the cohesion but also the hostility of tribal groups. It is indeed a melancholy fact that all the root causes of tension in our contemporary world, all the disputes that lead to enmity and war, can be found equally well in tribal society. The characteristic state of the African interior when Western missionaries first explored it a hundred years ago was almost universal tribal warfare springing from the economic pressures of hunger and want or the political pressures of tribal aggrandizement.

These two great causes of conflict have differed only in form, not in essence, over the millennia of human existence. When one tribe takes over the hunting ground or the fishing reserves of another tribe, the motives are not much different from Hitler's when he dreamt of enslaving, for German use, the great granaries of the Ukraine. And where economic pressure is lacking, political ambition often takes its place. The tribe which is stronger in numbers and in coherence is tempted, in sheer pursuit of power, to impose its will upon a weaker neighboring group. The Ashantis press down to the sea, the Fulanis impose control on the Hausas, the Zulus sweep south, the Yaos sell their neighbors to the Arab slavers. Unknown chiefs of a thousand tribes were the predecessors of our Alexanders and Napoleons, of Tamerlane or Genghis Khan.

But in most parts of the world, tribal organization has now been left behind and the reasons for its passing are almost as various as the history of man itself. Here I would like to mention three or four causes of change and development, each decisive in the unfolding of human destiny. The first could almost be called the origin of civilization itself. It occurred when the need for more organized and more developed methods of cultivation imposed unity upon a number of different families and groups and tribes. It is significant that more elaborate political, administrative, and technical methods were first evolved in the Nile valley, along the two great rivers of Mesopotamia, and in the basins of the Indus and the Yellow River. The mighty masses of water, flooding and receding, offered opportunities for cultivation and risks of disaster that could be mastered only by the highly organized efforts of very large numbers of people. Administration in the grand manner was a necessity, and in these first centers of civilization, arising in the third and second millennia before Christ, political cohesion was reinforced by an often elaborate bureaucracy.

Another method of change has been the spread of large and prolific tribal groupings by peaceful settlement. The diffusion of the Slav peoples through Eastern Europe, through Great Russia, and in recent centuries eastwards to Siberia is the essential underpinning of the modern Soviet state. The children of Han—the sturdy tribes of Northern China—also multiplied and possessed the land as they moved southwards from the Yellow River. And although their migrations occurred in post-tribal times, we might also note the wave of relatively peaceful settlement that has been at work in the last three centuries in North America.

But over most of the world, it is the third method of change that has put an end most decisively to tribal organization. Conquest has been the greatest lever of change in human history. We may pray it is not still so today—but of the past, there can be no question. Large groups absorb the smaller tribes in the area, and a paramount chief is on a fair way to establish a kingdom. The conquered tribes keep a subsidiary existence, possibly as vassals, and the kingdom is likely to go through a feudal phase. Loyalty to the tribe is transformed into loyalty to the leader or the dynasty. The language of the conquerors is imposed, or there arises from conqueror and conquered together a new common tongue. The area of cohesion is thus enlarged, and for long periods of history the dominant political form is the dynastic state or the dynastic empire.

The form of change I would like to examine more closely at this point is the rise of nationalism in the modern sense. For this, we must follow the development of Western society in its cradle of the Mediterranean and Western Europe. Here nationalism, as we understand it today, was born. In Western Europe a particular set of coincidences—racial and geographical—set human history moving on a new track.

The early structure of Western Europe, after the collapse of the Roman Empire, was that of tribal groups coalescing, after a series of conquests, into feudal kingdoms. As the Middle Ages advanced, three of these groups began to take on a recognizably national form. The tribes of Gaul had been conquered by Caesar and given a Latinized speech. Under the feudal divisions of the land—between English overlords, Capetian monarchs, and Burgundian vassals—the mass of people began to speak a recognizable French, and this linguistic area had fairly well-defined geographical frontiers—on the Atlantic, on the Pyrenees, and along the Alps.

Only one frontier was indeterminate—in Alsace Lorraine—and has been, as a result, one of the most unstable frontiers of recent history with an unenviable record of invasions and counterinvasions on into our own day. But by the end of the Middle Ages—say, the late fourteenth century—France had become conscious of itself as a big national group speaking the French tongue, and possibly the chief reason for this self-aware-ness was the amount of time the French had to spend fighting the English next door. Nothing so concentrates one's national feeling as being aware of somebody else's.

England, after the Norman conquest, followed some-thing of the same cycle. The language of the French conquerors was fused with the native Anglo-Saxon to form the English tongue, and the very fact of being an island created early the sense of cohesion and separate-ness from other lands.

> This happy breed of men, this little world,
> This precious stone set in the silver sea,
> Which serves it in the office of a wall
> Or as a moat defensive to a house,
> Against the envy of less happier lands,
> This blessed plot, this earth, this realm,
>   this England.

The glowing nationalism with which Shakespeare in-vested his panegyric drew not a little of its warmth from his sense of the long struggle against the "less happier lands"—against France in his historical plays, against Spain in his own day. The cohesion of each national group was being reinforced all the time by the consciousness of its neighbor's nationalism.

Spain is the last of the trio. Its sense of a common national destiny was forged in the struggle to turn the Arab conquerors out of the Iberian Peninsula and was reinforced by Latinized speech and the frontiers of sea and mountain which cut it—and the Portuguese enclave—off from the bulk of Europe. These three countries reached the threshold of the modern world with a unique coincidence of language and frontier. To the sense of historical continuity, of destiny shared and memories reaching back into a common past, was added the firmest of cements—a common tongue. The idea that this might be the strongest element of cohesion within the state began to enter the consciousness of mankind.

II

Language alone is not, of course, enough to explain the rise of modern nationalism. Even language is a shorthand for the sense of belonging together, of sharing the same memories, the same historical experience, the same common cultural and imaginative heritage. When, in the eighteenth century, nationalism began to take form as a modern movement, its forerunners in many parts of Europe were not soldiers and statesmen but scholars and poets who sought to find in ancient legends and half-forgotten folksongs the "soul" of the nation. But it was language that enshrined the memories, the common experience, and the historical record.

Nor could the sense of common tongue and culture have become the political battering-ram that it is in our own times if it had not been inextricably bound up with the modern political and economic revolutions of the West—the political drive for democracy and the economic revolution of science and industry.

Three thousand years ago, in one small area of the Mediterranean world, there came a break with the earlier traditions of state-building, which were all despotic. The dominance of a strong local tribe or conquest by foreign groups had turned the old fragmented tribal societies into centralized dynastic imperial states in which the inhabitant was subject absolutely to the ruler's will. But in the Greek city-state, for the first time, the idea was formulated that a man should govern himself under law, and that he should be not a subject but a free citizen.

After the post-Roman collapse, it re-emerged as a seminal idea in the development of later European history. Even in the Middle Ages, before there were any fully articulated democratic systems, two or three of the essential foundations of democracy had appeared. The rule of law was recognized. The right of the subject to be consulted had called into being the parliaments and "estates" of the fourteenth century. And the possibility of a plurality of power—through State, through Church, through Royal boroughs and free municipalities—mitigated the centralizing tendencies of government. It was, in fact, for a restoration of these rights after the Tudor interregnum that the first modern political revolution, the English civil war, was fought.

If a man had a right to take part in his own government, it followed logically that his government could not be arbitrarily controlled from elsewhere. It was useless to give him representation if it did not affect the true center of power. The American Revolution symbolized the connection between the rights of the citizen and the rights of the state. The free citizen had a right to govern himself, *ergo* the whole community of free citizens had a right to govern itself. This was not yet modern nationalism. The American people did not see themselves as a national group but as a community of free men "dedicated to a proposition." But within two decades, the identification had been made.

The French Revolution, proclaiming the Rights of Man, formed the new style of nation. The *levée-en-masse* which defeated the old dynastic armies of Europe was the first expression of total national unity as the basis of the sovereign state. Men and nations had equally the right to self-determination. Men could not be free if their national community was not.

The same revolution quickly proved that the reverse might not be true. The nation could become completely unfettered in its dealings with other states while enslaving its own citizens. In fact, overglorification of the nation might lead inevitably to the extinction of individual rights. The citizen could become just a tool of the national will, of the so-called "general will." But in the first explosion of revolutionary ardor, the idea of the Rights of Man and of the Rights of the Nation went together. And, formally, that is where they have remained. At the end of the First World War, it was the world's leading democratic statesman, Woodrow Wilson, who wrote the right of self-determination, the right of national groups to form their own sovereign government, into the Peace Treaties and at no time in human history have so many independent national states been formed as after the Second World War.

We turn now to the economic aspects of modern nationalism. It was not certain, when the Industrial Revolution first gathered momentum in Britain, that the new economic forces would reinforce the political drive of nationalism. Many Englishmen thought not. They shared Tennyson's vision of commerce uniting the nations in a web of common interests and leading to "the parliament of man, the federation of the world." Free trade would enable each area to produce what it was most fitted to produce and to exchange its wares freely the world over.

But the vision did not survive much beyond the middle of the nineteenth century. The unification of the German-speaking principalities in a single Reich was preceded by a customs union. Tariffs kept out competing British goods and enabled German industry to draw level and ahead. Thus there came about in Germany a complete coincidence of the national and economic boundary at a time when nationalism was new and feverishly conscious of its role. At the same time, the industrialization of the country drew all classes into dependence upon the new unified economy. It was now no longer the interests of a few merchants that were at stake in the defense of the national economy. Everyone's livelihood depended upon it. If it was threatened, so were they. Wars had been fought in the past to safeguard marginal commercial advantages. What might not be done now to defend economic interests that were felt to be total? The answer was given in 1914 and again in 1939.

One of the most vivid descriptions of how nationalism grew in force and intensity in the nineteenth century has been given by Professor Toynbee. He describes the old political mold of dynastic states based upon royal families—the German principalities, for instance, or the Hapsburg Empire—and points out that in the nineteenth and twentieth centuries, two molten forces of change were poured into this old vessel. On one side there flowed in the full force of democracy, the passionate conviction that everyone had the right to play a part in the community and that the community should therefore represent the citizens and their interests. On the other, the heady brew of economic nationalism was added, the belief that with industrialization everybody's livelihood was now at stake in the preservation of the national economy.

This sudden, passionate increase in the interest felt by everyone in the nation led, as we shall see, to an immense enhancement of its capacity and energy and ability to undertake great communal efforts. But it also led to a tremendous and terrifying enhancement of hostility. No sooner was some interest of the group thought to be threatened from outside than the whole life of the community was felt to be at stake. And on these fears could be built so terrifying a battery of hatred, such a demonology of distrust and enmity that the nationalism of the nineteenth century led on to the total irrationality of National Socialism in our own time—and we still cannot be certain that the devils are exorcised.

III

From all this it will be clear that the development of nationalism is a recognizable, historical process. It happened in certain countries, it happened in a certain way, and it created a certain mood which became embodied in the national idea. With the means of communication open to the modern world, an idea developed in one place can quickly become the possession of all mankind. What is certain is that, in the twentieth century, nationalism, the historical product of certain political institutions, geographical facts, and economic developments in Western Europe, has swept around the world to become the greatest lever of change in our day.

We see it at the United Nations where, in the course of eleven short years, the number of sovereign states based upon the principle of nationhood has grown by three score and more. As I have pointed out, it is unprecedented in human history that such a number of separate, autonomous, sovereign nations should come into being in so short a space of time.

Perhaps the force of nationalism can better be gauged by its effect on established states than by its stimulus to the creation of new ones. When the American Revolution set up a government in the United States, it was not a nationalist government. It was a government, we have seen, dedicated to a proposition—that all men are equal. Freedom, not nationalism, would be its principle of organization. People would go to America not to become Americans but to be free. And yet in a hundred and fifty years that have passed since then, we cannot, I think, avoid the conclusion that while America has maintained its dedication to the great constitutional principles of its origin, it has also developed a distinct nationalism. It is, of course, a society in which an immense number of different peoples and races have, in fact, found a new sense of community; but out of the melting pot comes a type that is American in the nationalist sense.

The Russian Revolution, too, attempted to establish a state on ideological foundations alone. The new society was not Russian. It was the vanguard of the embattled proletarians of the world. In those days, neither Lenin nor Trotsky believed that the revolution could succeed in Russia unless it spread simultaneously all through Europe, and probably all around the world as well. In the early days, what was set up in Russia was the bridgehead of a new revolutionary system.

But in the last forty years and, in particular, since the announcement of "socialism in one country" by Stalin in 1928, we have witnessed, flowing into the revolutionary channels scoured out in the Soviet Union, the immense patriotic fervor of an older Russian nationalism. Stimulated by the people's heroic defense of their land in the last world war, the sense of Russian interests, of Russian power and pride, is fully as strong now as any surviving revolutionary principle. Communism has, indeed, become almost as much an instrument of Russian state power as was the pan-Slavism of the Czars.

This triumph of nationalism over two of the greatest ideological upheavals in all history suggests to me that it is still the strongest, most pervasive force of our day. There are, however, a few signs that it is beginning to spend itself a little and beginning to give ground to other concepts. And it is significant that these changes are to be remarked in Western Europe, first home of modern, industrialized, democratic nationalism and also the arena where the worst consequences of this type of nationalism have been worked out.

Europe's ghastly feuds, which we might well call the tribal wars of modern man, have led to a disgust with the extreme forms of nationalism. A new and absorbing struggle is in progress between the old concept of France, of Germany, of Italy, of Holland, and of Belgium as separate, sovereign, absolutely autonomous states and a new concept of supranational communities; a new sense that they must work together if they are to survive.

Behind the talk of political and economic union in Europe today there is in many hearts a sense of disillusion, a revulsion from the consequences of perfervid nationalism. The chance that this is the sign of a new trend, of a new seminal idea, is made all the more plausible by the place of its emergence—Western Europe, where national communities have been longest in being and have worked the longest havoc with each other.

But this is no more than a possibility. At the moment I would say that, looking around our modern world with its changing institutions, its social and economic developments, and its new forms of growth, we are perfectly justified in saying that nationalism is by far the strongest political force with which we have to reckon.

IV

What, then, are we to make of this force? How should we judge it? What are the credit and debit entries in the nationalist ledger? Perhaps the first thing to be said is that we have to give nationalism the respect which it is always wise to give to facts. The national community clearly seems to be one of the ways in which human beings naturally articulate their political institutions once they move on from the earlier patterns of tribal society.

It may be that this is a premature judgment. The two or three hundred years of the nation state are a short period on which to base generalities compared with the millennia of the human span. Yet most nation states have roots that go back far beyond modern nationalism and, if we take the last 2,000 years of relatively developed civilized history, I think it is possible to say that there are signs of certain national units emerging as permanent groupings within the human race. Perhaps "permanent personalities" would express the fact better. There is a recognizable French or German style.

This point can, I think, be strengthened by an illustration neither from Europe nor from modern history. Soon after the birth of Christ—under the Han dynasty in China—the people of Annam were incorporated into the Chinese Empire and there they remained for a thousand years. From the beginning of the Christian era to the end of the ninth century, Annam was part of China, and I need hardly underline the fact that the Chinese are probably, of all conquerors, the most able to absorb other groups into their culture, which is notoriously "spongelike" or absorptive. The steady spread of Chinese society has been by a succession of annexations during which alien organisms have been absorbed into the system and turned into Chinese.

But at the end of a thousand years, the Annamites withdrew their allegiance, left the Empire and returned to being Annamites, which they have been ever since. In other words, the most cohesive, the most pervasive, the most absorptive imperial system in the history of mankind was unable to absorb a small neighboring people even after a thousand years of imperial control. They emerged as they went in—a recognizable national unit.

The nation, then, is a normal, possibly *the* normal

personality for human groups in the post-tribal stage and this basic fact, without elaboration, could, I suggest, be placed on the credit side of the balance sheet. It would be appalling indeed to imagine a world without national differences, without variety either of culture or of temperament, without the possibility of counterpoint and harmony in international life. The picture of humanity all of the same type, all under the same institutions, all possibly wearing blue Chinese dungarees is a nightmare of which you can get a faint foretaste from modern air travel. You can go from airport to airport all around the world and wonder where you are. They all look exactly alike. This standardizing tendency in our modern industrial system makes one all the more eager to cling to any sense of separate personality, culture, or tradition. National differences offer the best hope for variety and difference and in this measure foster taste and creativeness in the midst of our industrial uniformities.

Another positive value of nationalism is that it can be powerfully mobilized to achieve great communal tasks. This point is well illustrated, I believe, by the contrasting histories of two great Far Eastern countries, China and Japan. They both, at different times, underwent a terrific battering at the hands of European traders who sought to open up their markets to Western commerce. In the sixteenth century the Japanese responded by closing themselves up to all outside contacts and for over two hundred years maintained a policy of rigorous exclusion of virtually all foreign influence.

When, in the course of the last century, European pressure began to be heightened against China, the country could not make such a firm response. Its internal political weakness was growing. The Manchu dynasty was crumbling, and in the nineteenth century, foreigners began to exploit this weakness for their own commercial gain. As a result, much of the early modernization and industrial development of China was undertaken by foreigners and under foreign influence.

The later development of the two countries was conditioned by these early differences. By the middle of the nineteenth century, it became clear to the Japanese that safety no longer lay in seclusion. The only way in which they could check Western penetration into their still feudal economy would be to take up the task of modernization for themselves. After 1870, Japanese reformers and modernizers took over the entire economic and political system and remodeled it on the modern Western industrial pattern. The task could be done because the years of withdrawal had preserved the sense of a single national community. The leaders could draw on national energies unconfused by foreign occupation or by internal divisions resulting from occupation.

The Chinese, on the contrary, resembled one of their own great junks, dismasted and running rudderless before a tornado. Internally they were split. Parts of China's nascent economy were under total foreign control. No national energies could be mobilized, for there was no sense of unity or leadership. From the Taiping revolt to the Communist revolution, China spent nearly a century in search of a political unity and national will that would make possible the vast effort of modernization needed to bring half a billion people into the modern world.

Before we leave Asia, I might cite another example. In one sense, India was more fortunate than China. In India, foreign rule brought a framework of administrative order and unity. The country was not simply frittered away between foreign and local rivalries. It gained a solid underpinning of order and domestic peace under the British. Yet in spite of much economic development, especially in transport and irrigation, British rule in the twentieth century was not and could not be dynamic. Nothing so far-reaching and energetic as the first and second Indian five-year plans could have been introduced save under genuine, indigenous national leadership. Foreign rule would always blunt and divert national energies. It could not direct them towards great constructive and cooperative ends.

Thus foreign rule, however enlightened, is no substitute for vigorous national leadership. Yet it must also be admitted that foreign rule is one of the principal means by which strong national consciousness is fostered. This has always been so. Nothing so concentrates the loyalty of the tribe as the need to oppose some threat offered by another. But modern nationalism of the Western model is much more than the instinctive readiness of the group to defend its own integrity. It is, as we have seen, a fully articulated philosophy of international relations. People always have resented being ruled by foreigners. Now their inalienable right not to be so governed is recognized. The world community must respect these rights just as domestic government accepts the rights of individual citizens.

Nationalism in this sense is a manifestation of the Western search for freedom under law as *the* organizing principle of human society. As such, it is the most powerful dissolvent of empires the world has ever known. And I am not thinking only of the energy it gives to those who seek to be free. I am thinking, too, of its effect upon the governors.

Up to the threshold of our day, the passing of empires has always been a time of trouble and misery. The links have only been dissolved to the accompaniment of violence, destruction, and human agony. Often the result has been what Marx foresaw as "the common ruin of the contending parties." But with the ideal of self-governing nationalism a new principle entered the comity of nations as part of the common political patrimony of mankind. Colonial leaders have seized on it, but—from the point of view of amity and the peaceful transfer of power —it is even more important that imperial powers have also recognized it. And just as one element in the idea of self-governing nationalism can be traced back to the ancient Greeks, the readiness of Western imperialism to give ground can also be linked to the classical founders of human freedom.

Alone among the active, vigorous trading people of

the Mediterranean in the millennium before Christ, the Greek city states did not use their pre-eminence to found an empire. When Greek interests and Greek trade began to spread, the Greeks set up not a single colonial system but other independent self-governing Greek city states. And when at various times, under the pressure of the vast Persian empire, the suggestion was made that the Greek cities would be advised to fuse their sovereignty under centralized leadership, the decisive argument was that although it might be better and more efficient to set up a large centralized system, it would not in the least resemble the political organization the Greeks knew and loved—the "polis"—the city in which all citizens had their vote and their stake. They would rather, therefore, have independent cities in a loose confederation such as the Delian League than anything resembling an organized, centralized Greek imperial state. It was not until the collapse of freedom at home and the disappearance of self-government in the free city-states, that a leader arose in the person of Alexander (with our odd habit of naming all conquerors great, we call him "the Great"), who created a vast empire based upon Greek power and the extension of Greek culture. But in the great days of the Greek city states, they found themselves unable to form a centralized empire because, basically, they did not believe in despotic control at home.

In our own day, one of the factors in the swift rise and equally swift disappearance of the European empires of the eighteenth and nineteenth centuries is that they were controlled by metropolitan communities in process of becoming increasingly democratic. The dictatorial principle upon which these empires were inevitably based could not be maintained in face of the growth of self-government among the metropolitan people. It is difficult to be completely democratic at home and run systems overseas which are not. This contradiction has worked itself out so quickly that in the last fifteen years we have witnessed throughout the old colonial areas—apart from one or two troublespots—either the transformation or virtual disappearance of those empires that are governed by nations with democratic principles at home.

This is, I am sure, a relationship of cause and effect. Those who believe in national self-determination for themselves are compelled, whether some groups in the community like it or not, to recognize it for others. It is no coincidence that the one great power in the world that has had no history save under free government—the United States—has been, in relation to its power and scale, remarkably free of expansionist policies or adventures. Excursions into foreign conquest—as in the Caribbean or the Philippines—have always aroused such opposition at home that they could not be pursued wholeheartedly and were sooner or later abandoned. This settled tendency cannot be dismissed as simply a function of America's ample continental living space; in the past, largeness has usually been a temptation to become larger still. It must also be attributed to America's adherence to the principle that nations, like individuals, have the inalienable right to be free.

This brings us to the interesting query whether the two large remaining empires under despotic government—the Russian Empire and the Chinese Empire—are likely to undergo the dissolvent process of modern nationalism. Have their dictatorial systems enough power to resist erosion? Is modern Communism, with its drive to create a closely knit industrial community, a sufficient counterforce? Here we are in the field of guesswork, and all I can put forward is my own guess. The Chinese Empire, which has been formed over millennia of slow growth through the cultural penetration of smaller tribal groups by the highly evolved civilization and language of the sons of Han, is now a nation and not an empire. The consolidation of the Chinese Empire took place so long before the development of modern ideas of nationalism and self-government that the internal groups are now thoroughly absorbed. There are, no doubt, frontier areas where the absorption is not complete. The Communists have had to make concessions in Tibet and Sinkiang. There has been some recent regrouping of local units in the South so as to bring men and women of related clans together in the same province. But these are on the margins. China is in essence a vast, unified nation.

The Russian Empire is much more diverse. Along its southern boundaries, it controls great numbers of

Turkish-speaking peoples, and has sought to consolidate the process of conquest that went on under the Czars as recently as the eighteenth and nineteenth centuries. Soviet colonial policy has combined highly centralized Great Russian political and economic control with the encouragement of local education, local language, and local culture. In Europe, rising living standards and greater opportunities led, as we have seen, to increased nationalist feeling. Will this be the consequence in such areas as Khirgizia and Khazakstan—or even the Ukraine? May the process even be encouraged by the measure of economic decentralization which Mr. Khrushchev has recently introduced?

I would not care to be dogmatic. In lands where modern education and modern industrialization have been thrust forward on strictly Communist lines, it may be that the sense of belonging to a great ideological community will be sufficient to counteract the fact that the community is still overwhelmingly run by Great Russians. Perhaps for some centuries yet, the Russians may be the Romans of this vast modern empire, building, expanding, giving law and order under a despotic government, admitting lesser peoples to equal opportunity and citizenship and creating a loyalty that transcends local separatism. Against it must be set the instability of the local governments in the fringe republics and the frequency with which the Communists denounce "bourgeois nationalism." In short, we do not know—although I myself incline to believe that the Russians may be able to consolidate a cultural and economic community in Soviet Asia much as the Chinese have done in their vast land.

But in one area I think we can agree that the Russian empire has little chance of becoming permanent. In Eastern Europe Russian control has been extended over countries which have centuries of separate national consciousness behind them. Some of them owed their deliverance from earlier empires to the triumph of the idea of national self-determination in Europe after 1918. Countries like Czechoslovakia or Poland—countries which have preserved their sense of national separateness through previous periods of imperial domination—are uncomfortable cement in any new or lasting imperial structure. The disturbances and upheavals in Eastern Europe in recent years are a sign that, whatever the form of empire, the desire for national self-determination still acts as a dissolvent of external bonds. Behind the protestations of "proletarian solidarity" still lies the indigestible fact of the satellites' suppression and Russian control.

V

So much for the strengths and benefits derived from the modern national spirit. If I refer to the drawbacks only briefly at this point it is because they form the substance of many of the international problems we are to review.

In its domestic aspect, the disadvantage of nationalism on the European model is that it presupposes a common language and a reasonably homogeneous society. But there are parts of the world where these conditions hardly prevail. In Eastern Europe, for instance, the principle of self-determination dissolved the Austro-Hungarian empire into its component nationalities, but no frontiers that could be devised would have put all the members of all the groups tidily inside their allotted frontiers. You could not construct a Rumanian state without including a Magyar minority. Ruthenian groups found themselves in three states. German enclaves were everywhere. Thus emerged a problem of minorities, of their rights, of their dubious loyalties, of their downright mistreatment by the majority. And it must be admitted that many parts of the world tend toward the Eastern European pattern of intermingling nationalities rather than the clear divisions and frontiers of Western Europe.

Another factor in this confusion is the number of states which have come into being in the last dozen years by opting out of somebody else's empire. But often before they opted out, they had been brought together as a unit solely by the chance pattern of imperial conquest. The modern frontiers of Southeast Asia— where Thais and Karens and Mons and Kachins and Cambodians and Annamites and a dozen other small national and tribal groups live side by side—were determined more by the interaction of British and French colonial interests than by actual national divisions.

A glance at the map of West Africa shows how completely the colonizing energies of the British, the French, and the Germans at the turn of the century determined the frontiers of the new states. At times, tribal areas and frontiers coincided, but the more usual experience was that of the Ewes who found themselves divided for a considerable time by three different "national" frontiers, all of external colonial origin. The communities thus created could be "nationalist" in the sense of uniting in their desire to be rid of imperial control. They were not equally nationalist in the sense of sharing common memories, common allegiances, and a common tongue.

This is not to say that nationhood cannot be achieved where this substratum is lacking. Switzerland is an obvious example of three language groups coexisting in a single state. But the more likely outcome is that tension and suspicion and lack of trust will disrupt the community's cohesion.

This risk is unhappily increased by modern democratic methods. By the principle of "one man, one vote" and the adoption of majority rule, minorities fear to be perpetually outvoted by a majority of another race or tongue. Take, for instance, the case of Ceylon. For hundreds of years, Ceylon has been more or less divided between the Tamils, who speak one language, and the Singhalese, who speak another. There has been some friction but, on the whole, the country was free of communal discord, especially so long as both groups could agree on the desirability of ending British imperial control. But since the achievement of independence and the introduction of adult suffrage, the Tamils have feared to be outvoted. They have become conscious of themselves as a minority and their fears and efforts at self-preservation have aroused the communal feeling of the Singhalese. In recent years there has been rising tension in what was once a quiet and friendly society.

Or let us take the example of the Indian Union. The idea of India as a nation state, fostering Indian pride and Indian nationalism, drew much of its strength from the struggle to be rid of the British. But inside India there are two major language groups and something like twenty-six major languages. In addition, there may be six hundred or more local languages. Can this welter of tongues be molded into sufficient unity to preserve the Union as a whole, especially when a number of states in the federation—states such as the Punjab or Bengal—are to be based as far as possible upon a coincidence of language and frontiers? The communal riots between Gujarati and Maharati in Bombay were a warning how high passions can run on the local national issue. Without some common tongue to reinforce the broad cultural and religious Hindu tradition, the Indian Union could founder into a confusion of competing linguistic states. This is a danger which modern nationalism—and modern voting procedures—do nothing to minimize. On the contrary, the stronger the nationalism, the greater the risk.

But the greatest danger of nationalism in our modern world is that its loyalties are too narrow. It does not admit of obligations beyond its own frontiers, of rights and duties which transcend the state. Yet in a world where space is conquered, where Sputniks circle above us and we can move faster than sound, we cannot confine our interests and responsibilities behind our own frontiers. That way leads to suicide for all states, great or small. This point will recur so often that it need not be elaborated here.

VI

Perhaps the most useful summary that one can give of all these facets of nationalism is to trace them in the development of one strong modern movement—Arab nationalism—which, at the moment, spins at the center of the world's political maelstrom.

When the Arab tribes burst into the Mediterranean and Levantine world twelve hundred years ago, they carried with them a language and a faith. These were planted from the shores of the Atlantic to the mountains of India. After the first heroic period of sweeping conquest, the Arabs fell apart into separate kingdoms—in Cordova, in Tunis, in Egypt and Baghdad. But Arab linguistic unity remained while the Moslem faith spread outward to India and farther Asia. Then came eclipse, and for centuries—centuries of torpor—the Arab lands were subject to the Turkish Empire.

The first stirrings of modern Arab nationalism began

when Napoleon carried the ideas of the French Revolution to Egypt. Egypt it was that took the first tentative
steps towards modernization. Then came the phase—
typical of Central and Eastern Europe—when Arab
scholars and poets, above all in the Christian Lebanon,
rediscovered the glories of Arabic literature and the
Arab tongue. These men were precursors of Arab poli-
ticians who, early this century, began to plot the overthrow of the Turks.

The first setback to this early nationalism came after
1918 when, in return for helping Britain and France to
defeat the Turks, the Arabs received not the independence they expected but inclusion in the British
and French colonial system and the establishment of
a Jewish enclave in Palestine. Between the wars, Arab
nationalism came more and more to be directed to one
overriding aim—getting rid of the Western intrusion.
The Second World War called a truce. After it, the
pressure began again, and it is impossible to compre-
hend the troubled Middle East if one underestimates
the growing fervor of the Arab nationalist idea or its
tendency to side against the Western Powers. It is
rooted in a common tongue. It calls on distant but
heroic memories. It has had external Western control
to throw off. It still suffers the irritant of Israel. All
these factors are enough to bring it to fever pitch.

Equally it shows the strength and weakness of nationalism. It requires energy and effort to wake an area
from the slumbers of centuries. If vast oil revenues are

to be used for genuine modernization, if Egypt's appalling problem of overpopulation is to be met, if the area is to be dragged up from some of the lowest living standards in the world, it is difficult to think of any force other than genuine nationalism to give peoples the faith and energies and courage to undertake such tremendous tasks.

But the dark face of nationalism has also shown itself. It has yet to be proved that "Arabism" as such can provide the cement for communities as diverse in interest as the oil-rich and oil-hungry Arab states. In Lebanon, with its very large Christian minority, or Iraq with its Kurds, insistence on Arab nationalism could undermine the state itself.

But these internal problems are nothing compared with the recklessness of Arab nationalism as an international force. No international society can survive peacefully if nations organize their energies on the basis of so much hatred of other groups. It is hardly a praiseworthy achievement to keep the world on the brink of war. No local aim can be worth the risk of general destruction. In its blind disregard of other rights and interests, in its total absorption in its own ambitions, Arab nationalism may end not by recreating the Middle East but by ending the whole human experiment.

These, then, in concrete form, are the grandeurs and servitudes of the nationalist idea.

Chapter Two

Industrialism

ALL around the world today, nations and societies are preoccupied with the problems involved in industrialism. Old established industrial societies have their own difficulties of stability, of growth, of balance between consumption and saving. But the great majority of the human race still live in more or less pre-industrial societies, and their problem is to make the decisive change from their traditional, largely static economic methods to the new possibilities of dynamism inherent in modern technology. This is the crucial economic revolution we must examine first of all.

In the political order, as we have seen, tribalism is the starting point of human history. And there is a corresponding economic phase of development. At some point, the roving human groups, hunting in the forest and fishing in the streams, learned how to make plants grow and how to tame animals. Settled agriculture became possible, and all over the world, wherever soil and rainfall favored it, tribal life came to be built upon "subsistence farming"—these words simply mean that farmers produce almost entirely for themselves, to meet their own needs, and are little concerned with production for an outside market.

In this early phase of agriculture, the land, generally speaking, is held in common by the tribe, by the clan, sometimes by the village; individual families are allotted land for use, not ownership—even though the same pieces of land tend to be handed down within the same family. The system has some great social virtues. The major activities—harvesting, sowing—call out the communal energies of the whole group and tribal, or village, cohesion guarantees everyone food and a share in the community.

Nor, within limits, is the system wasteful. Many African tribes allot to each family enough land to allow long periods of fallow during which the fertility of the soil is built up again by natural regeneration. For thousands of years, Indian and Chinese peasants have kept their land in good health, manuring, watering, terracing, with meticulous care for the soil.

(46)

But there are problems which subsistence agriculture cannot solve. If population rises, its chief resource is to bring more land under cultivation. But suppose there is no more land? The fallowing time is cut, the land is overfarmed, soil erosion and exhaustion set in. The pressure of family demands reduces the size of family holdings, the strips shrink, and for all the labor that goes into them, they become too small to produce effectively. These are the well-known cycles of subsistence agriculture which in small tribal communities such as Ruanda Urundi or in vast empires on the scale of China have brought recurrent crises of dislocation and disaster. And within the framework of largely static agriculture, there is no way out, once population exceeds resources. It is for this reason that the search for new land has been one of the underlying motives of conquest since history began.

There are ways out of the impasse and their discovery usually marks a new phase in human development. The secret lies in productivity—an obscure word for a crucial process—in making the soil produce more for the same amount of work and effort. All agriculture, of course, depends upon human ingenuity, upon the application of brainpower to the resources of soil and climate. But there were and are obstacles in subsistence agriculture to the full-blooded pursuit of new techniques. Where the land is held in common, the innovator will not gain directly from a new usage. The individual stimulus is lacking. And this is another way of stressing the conservatism of static agricultural societies.

It is in part a fruitful conservatism, since it is conserving practices and traditions which ensure good husbandry. In Tanganyika, for instance, the first European settlers scoffed at the African gardens where pulse and roots, vegetables and grain, all grew together. It did not take a long experience of European planting in open rows to realize that the matted African vegetation had provided essential protection for the soil.

But the conservatism also acts as a brake on essential change. Take, for instance, the effect of progressively subdividing the land available for family cultivation. There is no hope of greater output unless holdings can be consolidated, and this is one of the problems facing such tribal areas as the native reserves in Kenya or Southern Rhodesia. But the tenacity of old customs is underlined by the fact that the consolidation of farms is one of the aims in agricultural reform in France today —in other words, in a modern Western industrial community. It is equally a vital element in land reform in India. Thus the problems which beset the passage from conservative farming to modern techniques of agriculture are new and old, local and universal. And perhaps for a community such as Ghana, which faces this necessary transformation, there is encouragement in the thought that all manner of peoples and societies have gone along this route and left lessons and warnings and hopes behind them; and Ghana in its turn will now experiment and innovate—sometimes failing, sometimes succeeding—and thus add its experience to the common knowledge of mankind.

II

We come now to the various ways in which the original pattern of subsistence agriculture has been decisively altered. In its original tribal form, it produced food for the local group and did little more. There was no margin for an elaborate superstructure of government or culture, no surplus from which external authority could levy taxes for administration, for war, for the building of great cities and temples and the creation of a complicated urban civilization. The first great change came with the elaboration of irrigated agriculture in the great river basins—on the Nile and the Euphrates, the Indus and the Yellow River. In all these areas there was an enormous flow of water which, if it could only be regulated, would bring much greater productivity, much greater powers of growth from the soil—and which, unchecked, would continue to bring recurrent catastrophe. As we have already remarked, it is in these areas where there was a challenge to ingenuity, a challenge to man to apply his intelligence to his resources in a new way, that the whole experiment of civilization, as we know it, began.

For what we find is not simply an agricultural revolution; we also find vast developments in technology, and in applied science. In learning to control the waters of their rivers, the early Egyptians and Sumerians had to accomplish many other things as well; for instance, they had to have precise reckoning of how much soil would be covered by the rising waters, and in all probability it was in measuring the soil for this purpose that geometry and trigonometry were evolved—all the techniques of measurement upon which modern science is based.

They also had to estimate when the rains could be relied upon to come, and how long they would last. A scientific study of climate led to the first experiments in astronomy, the first careful observation of the seasons, the first attempt to measure solar change. Thus the application of water power to farming entailed not only an agricultural revolution, it brought with it a technological and scientific revolution, and these made possible the elaborate political structures of the first post-tribal states. Agriculture and the land tax were still the basis of their culture, but far more developed human activities could be erected upon them.

It is, however, usual in the human story for some great advantage to be purchased at the price of an equal drawback. So it proved in the great archaic civilizations. The systems of water-control, involving thousands upon thousands of cubic tons of water, could only be managed by very large-scale planning and a very large-scale bureaucracy. And it is no coincidence, I think, that all these early societies tended in their very structure to be dictatorial. The work was so complicated and depended upon so much human cooperation of a highly organized kind that it could be accomplished only under discipline and obedience. In such conditions, the claims of society, not of the individual, would naturally be emphasized, and in these early experiments in civilization, there is no sense of the inhabitants living as citizens with rights as free men.

This fact has, I think, more than historical interest. Down to our own day we can observe the distinction between societies which are dedicated to planning in a detailed, centralized fashion and societies which are more fluid and flexible. The roots of this distinction long antedate Communism or democracy. It can be traced back thousands of years to the societies which were built up on the basis of large-scale irrigation and large managerial organization, and other societies which grew up within a less rigid framework.

The Greeks, whom we have already met in the guise of political innovators, underwent an economic revolution too. Their political contribution—a system based upon the concept of the citizen, participating in government and ruled by law—was matched by a dynamic response to their economic problems. Instead of remaining in their own, small, closed territories as their population outstripped their resources or embarking on the conquest of other people—the customary "solution"—they turned to international commerce instead. They specialized in the production of what we would now call cash crops—the olive tree and the vine—and on the fine workmanship of their artisans, especially the potters, and in return for these exports they imported the wheat their soil was too thin to produce sufficiently. One social result of this change was the predominance of independent farmers and of a mobile, volatile merchant class—men who would be likely, in sturdy independence, to seek an open, flexible type of society.

The Greek experiment did not last. It was overlaid first by the despotism of Alexander, and later, of the Roman world. And the Roman world, in its later economic organization, did, in fact, borrow much from the oriental systems of large-scale organization and planning. For a comparable coincidence of economic variety and political independence, we have to jump about a thousand years, to the history of Western Europe as the Middle Ages come to an end.

Perhaps the clearest way of describing this new phase of flexible and varied development is to compare Asia and Europe at this crucial time. In Asia the political forms were all despotic. China and India, the two great centers of advanced civilization, had well-centralized empires based on a large and effective bureaucracy whose chief task was to collect the land tax—or the grain levies—upon which the glories of the state depended. It is curious to recall that long after, in the Indian Civil Service under British rule, field officers were still called "collectors" because collecting the land tax had been the earlier governments' main concern.

These states were immensely wealthy in all the goods which men most prize as luxuries—gold, silver, precious stones, ointments and perfumes, fine silks and tapestries, elaborate armor, thoroughbred horses, swift animals of the chase. Yet for all this wealth, the merchants had not the influence of officials or landowners. Internal commerce was small in relation to agriculture. The self-sufficient Indians and Chinese were hardly concerned with external trade at all. And although Arab merchants sailed over all the Eastern seas, their wealth did not bring direct political influence or modify the absolute government of their Moslem leaders at home.

In Europe, political power was diffused. Christianity, rendering to Caesar the things that are Caesar's and to God the things that are God's, set up a central plurality of power. The resulting struggle of Emperor and Pope to achieve supremacy gave subordinate authorities—kings, princes, cities, communes—the leverage to increase their own authority. Europe was strung across with a constellation of sovereignties, great and small. Many of these owed some of their vigor—as the Greeks had done—to a growing merchant class. Unlike the great lands of Asia, Europe had to trade because Europe was not self-sufficient. In fact, Europe was poor, enclosed within one belt of temperate climate, with no precious metals in the soil. The European peoples had to look to the Levant and to Asia for the better things of life. Vigorous communities trading with the Orient produced the burghers and freedmen of the Italian city states and of free communes in Germany, England, and the Lowlands as both internal and external trade increased.

The wealth of the cities spread out to the country-side, to modify feudal subsistence agriculture. Rich men from the town bought land from impoverished lords—or married their daughters. Enterprising serfs, turned yeomen, took over their own land. The bustle and change of the cities, open to all manner of outside influences, affected the traditional conservatism of the farms. It is a fact that throughout the Middle Ages there were all manner of technological experiments in European agriculture—changing the yoke of the plow to suit the horse, not the ox, for instance, or setting up windmills like sailing ships across the land—both being applications of extra energy to traction, which is one of the bases of all technological change. Landlords were also innovators in diversifying their products—as we see from the introduction of wool into thirteenth-century England. In short, the old pattern of subsistence agriculture in Europe was broken not so much by one great change to a new highly efficient and highly centralized system but by myriad new spurts and experiments, based upon the activities of thousands of different centers of economic and political power.

At this stage, the contrast between Europe and Asia gave Europe no advantage in terms of wealth. As the Middle Ages ended, Asia was still the great center of political and economic power. In fact, odd as it is to recall the fact now, Europe at that time could never balance its books in its trade with Asia. The Europeans had little to offer in return for silks and jewels and perfumes. In the end, they always had to ship bullion back to Asia. In fact, as late as the eighteenth century, pamphlets were produced in Britain in which people denounced all these imports of Asian muslins and damask which were ruining Britain and draining it of gold to pay its Asian debts. It was almost like having a dollar gap, but in those days it was an "Asian gap" instead. As it turned out, the factor of wealth was less important than the factor of organization, of innovation, of drive and vitality. In fact, the very wealth of Asia served as a spur to the Europeans' further development. It was their determination to trade with the great centers of Asia without resort to Arab middlemen that sent the Portuguese around the Cape of Good Hope. It was the dream of "the gold which Cipangu [Japan] was ripening in its distant mines" that drew Columbus across the unknown wastes of the Atlantic. And the vast wealth that streamed in from the New World was one of the prime movers in Europe's decisive plunge into the industrial mode of production.

III

With the industrial revolution a process was set in motion which is steadily and inexorably changing the whole life of mankind. I do not mean by this that I am an economic determinist—that I believe everything we do to be conditioned by the kind of economy we live in. It is true that if there is a profound change in a community's method of carrying on its economy and conducting its daily economic life, then political and social institutions and even the people's whole way of looking at things will also be affected. But this does not prove, as the Marxists believe, that economic and productive relationships are primary and all the rest follows. Nowhere, in fact, can one see more clearly the complexity of cause and effect than in the beginnings of industrialization in Europe.

Let us take three instances in which political conditions and social beliefs did not reflect economic conditions but on the contrary helped to create them. The first is the crucial issue of saving. There have been rich merchant classes all through history—none richer, perhaps, than the Arab traders under the Caliphate. But it was from Calvinism that the merchants learned that it was meritorious on the one hand to work hard and build up a fortune and on the other not to spend it on luxuries and riotous living. Fortunes which were set to work to produce more fortunes through yet more work were one of the factors in building up the essential reserves of capital for industrial development. In less Puritan societies, much of the wealth would have been spent—on luxury or art or magnificence. In the West, the merchants were often the chief exponents of austerity. Not for nothing were the Quakers with their plain dress and plain speech among the fathers of modern banking.

The political atmosphere of Western Europe also gave encouragement to the commercial classes. Their successful struggles for self-government in the communes and kingdoms gave them more than political guarantees. It protected them against the expropriatory whims of the monarch. Oriental rulers were unpredictable and ruthless men in the matter of taxes and confiscations. If law depended on the prince's whim, so did property—an insecure basis and one which discourages plans for sustained accumulation.

But perhaps the most curious instance of the interplay between cultural and economic conditions concerns science and technology. The industrial revolution is inconceivable without applied science, and the turning of British minds in the seventeenth century from religious differences to a common pursuit of natural science was one of the pre-conditions of industrialism. Yet this shift of interest did not occur in either of the great and wealthy Oriental civilizations. Why?

In India one factor at least was a religion which taught the unreality of created things. There was thus little incentive to explore and define and measure the exact proportions of an illusion. In China, the study of natural phenomena became confused at an early date with necromancy and witchcraft. The Taoists taught a metaphysical doctrine, compounded elixirs to bestow immortality, and also observed natural phenomena closely. In the Confucian mind, Taoist observation and Taoist tomfoolery were damned together. Confucianism remained a science of human relations, not of material phenomena. Science never broke away from the imputation of magic. In short, it was no occupation for a gentleman, and gentlemen held the levers of Chinese power.

If I try to isolate three elements that were decisive in the transfer from agriculture to industry in the first industrial revolution—Britain's—and have proved an essential element in all the following ones, I do not, therefore, want to suggest that these are the only factors. There are a myriad psychological and historical and social pressures which give a particular stamp to each new industrial pattern. All that one can say is that whatever other factors play a part, three are decisive: an increased rate of saving, a revolution in productivity, and the transformation of agriculture.

The first two points hardly need to be elaborated. Even the most primitive community does a little saving. Not all the corn is consumed. Seed is set aside for the next harvest. It is saved in the literal sense and all saving is simply an extension of this—the postponement of consumption to ensure tomorrow's needs. Most undeveloped economies probably use about five percent of their national income for saving of this sort. Whether it is seed-corn for next year, mending the ditches and hedges around the farms or clearing new land for planting, a certain amount of capital work—saving work— is accomplished.

But this degree of saving does no more than keep the economy stable. If the population is increasing, more saving is needed to keep pace with new demand. The decisive change occurs when the economy, as it were, begins to get ahead of itself, when the saving not only ensures the same consumption next year but provides increased output which in turn promises even greater opportunities in years to come. Economists estimate that when a society begins to save and invest from twelve to fifteen percent of its national income, it has broken through the "sound barrier" between a static and a dynamic economy.

Some societies have pushed this percentage up even further, up to twenty and twenty-five percent of the national income. The Soviet Union has sustained this rate of saving over many decades. Production was primarily directed not to consumer goods but to more machines, more factories, more transport and more power, so that, all the time, the base of the economy was expanding and, with it, the power to produce a greater flow of goods in the future. But short of heroic measures on this scale, communities can ensure the expansion of their capacity by seeing to it that twelve to fifteen percent of their national income is devoted to the means of expanding future consumption and not simply to consumer goods such as textiles or food or movies or motorcars or anything that families consume and enjoy at once.

If income that is saved is to do its work of expanding the whole economy, the saving must, obviously, be productive. An immense amount of capital was devoted to building the pyramids, but the construction did not turn Egypt into a dynamic economy any more than air-conditioned palaces transform Saudi Arabia today. The range of goods which are productive in the true sense is, of course, vast. A new type of disease-resistant seed, an improved method of plowing, better layout in a workshop, better roads to take goods to market—all these things help men to produce more with the same amount of work, which is the essence of productivity. But the industrial revolution depends, perhaps more than on any other one factor, upon new supplies of energy. Putting more power behind each pair of hands is as old as civilization. Waterpower, horsepower, windpower—these were widely employed in earlier technologies. The full industrial revolution developed from steam power and has gone through electric power and oil power to the fateful nuclear power of our own day. Without power, there can be no industrialization, and the coal basins of the world are without exception the dirty cradles of modern industrialism.

So much for the scale and type of investment upon which industrialism depends. But the crucial question remains—where is it to come from? And, of course, it can, broadly speaking, only come from agriculture, since before industry, agriculture is the largest source of basic wealth. I am not forgetting the importance of trade. Export incomes have been a dynamic factor in many economies, not least in Ghana where existing capital funds for development—lavish funds for so small a population—have been derived from a careful management of the large funds earned by cocoa exports since the war. But many export incomes are in turn derived from farming—wool, for instance, or cotton, or the fantastic profits that used to be made by Western merchants engaged in the spice trade. Only mining stands on the same footing as agriculture as an original, pre-industrial source of wealth; certainly no one in Africa will underestimate the decisive part played by diamonds, gold, and copper in opening up the Continent. But even where export incomes earned from minerals are a primary source of saving, the transformation of agriculture is still a pre-condition of industrial advance.

So long as the bulk of the population remains on the land as subsistence farmers, a modern industrial society cannot develop. The farmers do not produce enough extra food to feed the workers needed in non-agricultural pursuits. Nor can men be released from the farms to the factories while so many hands are needed for traditional methods of cultivation. And farmers who are not producing anything for the market cannot go to the market as purchasers themselves. Local demand for consumer goods does not expand. There is thus no stimulus to local industrial production. Agriculture must, therefore, yield men and savings to the new industrialized, urbanized sectors if a modern and dynamic economy is to be achieved.

It is obvious that to transfer the output of one section of the community to another can lead to painful sacrifices. The early years of industrialism hitherto have been times of human dislocation and misery. The farming population work to provide the means of expansion elsewhere. If, at that time, their own production is stable, their standards must fall. Only if their techniques are improving and agricultural productivity rising can the transfer of resources be eased in some measure. The first nation to industrialize—Britain—was fortunate in having some margins with which to ease the transfer. The eighteenth century was a time of agricultural experiment and advance. Enlightened landowners such as "Turnip" Townshend or Coke of Norfolk invented new methods of winter feeding and crop rotation which greatly increased productivity in agriculture. The result was that as the Industrial Revolution gathered momentum in England, there was a growing agricultural margin from which savings could be transferred to the ironmasters and the spinners and weavers who were beginning to build up industry in Britain.

At the same time, let us not underestimate the immense hardship which the agricultural population of Britain underwent in those early days of industrialism when they came crowding in from the country into vast unsanitary towns where they worked sixty hours a week and died in misery. For at least forty years, between 1820 and 1860, the workers gained nothing from their new industrial way of life. This, incidentally, was the period which marks the crucial intellectual formation of Karl Marx. He saw in Britain that first, ugly, rough, brutal stage of the Industrial Revolution, and much that he says about capitalism was absolutely true of the 1840's and 1850's. During that period, the workers in the main did the saving in the strict sense of nonconsumption and the new wealth was devoted to expanding industry. It was only after 1860 that productivity of the new machines began to affect people's general standard of living. Real wages rose. The workers began to enjoy some of the fruits of the system. But in the early days, it was an ugly, bitter struggle.

Japan is another nation in which the transfer of savings from agriculture was mitigated by a sharp rise in agricultural productivity. Japan's performance in building a modern economy is, incidentally, one of the world's most extraordinary *tours de force* in industrialization. The Japanese, an overcrowded people on a small island with almost no mineral resources, were able to modernize their economy in twenty short years, and to produce the first fully industrial nation in Asia. And all this was done entirely on their own initiative. We have already seen how the sense of modern nationalism was one of the spurs to this change. But in the actual technique of launching industrialization, the interesting fact is that the Japanese took as their starting point an extensive land reform and a great drive to increase productivity. It did, in fact, double between 1870 and 1914. The working farmer had a stake in his land and his income was increasing. Even though a high percentage of the increased output was transferred, by way of taxation, into industry, a balance remained with the farmer. This he plowed back into his farm and also increased his own consumption. Men could be released from agriculture and the farmers also provided a market for consumer goods. Thus, in Japan, agriculture and industry expanded together.

If we wish to see the unhappy effects of an opposite development, we need only look to the Soviet Union. Soviet saving has been on a colossal scale but we can see today by hindsight that too much of the saving went into industry and too little into agriculture. Until Khrushchev introduced his series of agricultural reforms—of which the most far-reaching is the abolition of compulsory deliveries to the state—agriculture lagged behind the rapid rate of industrial advance. There were political reasons for this neglect. The Communists did not want too much prosperity and independence among farming people whose chief desire was to own land as private property. But the effect of holding down agriculture has affected everyone. It helps to account for lower standards of living and eating in both village and town.

Khrushchev's reforms may begin to fill the gap; yet it is significant that throughout Eastern Europe collectivization has been partially abandoned and private farming tolerated while the farmers are being encouraged to produce in some measure for the free market. Incentives are thus restored to agriculture after ten years of the Soviet pattern of a merciless squeezing of savings from the farms.

Yet Russia—like America—is fortunate in its resources. It is underpopulated. Khrushchev can order the ploughing of 75,000 acres of virgin land to redress the agricultural balance. But what happens when there are no margins? How do nations transfer savings from agriculture when their peasants are already on the smallest margins of consumption? This is the case in India and China, where the pressure of population on the land is so great that agricultural saving on a sufficient scale (and saving, always remember, means not consuming) could bring disaster. If you are living at the margin and you have to cut consumption, you simply die. And that, after all, is not a very cheerful prospect for the mass of agricultural people. This is the fundamental problem facing the vast communities of China and India. If governments save too much, they will save a great many people into the grave. And this is not meant metaphorically but literally and in fact. There is a limit beyond which you cannot depress consumption when consumption is already extremely depressed. Yet the only hope of getting away from ancestral poverty is to save—and save generously. No dilemma is more urgent or painful than this in lands where underdevelopment goes with overpopulation.

The political problem—whether a government ruling by consent can ever secure the needful saving—is a question to which we must return. Here I only want to

(65)

underline the special difficulties facing countries in which land and resources are already used up to—and beyond—the limit.

IV

When we come to the processes of industrialization, the variety is bewildering. It is as varied as the resources available in different communities. It is as variable as all the differing methods and principles of organization adopted by different states. Its essence may be the bringing together of workers in factory establishments, to transform raw materials or work them up further with the help of power and machines —but this broad generalization covers everything from the small cottage industry of Japan, in which single families work on components for large firms, to monsters such as the steel plant and iron foundry at Magnitogorsk, which are the largest in the world.

But there are one or two useful generalizations to be made, in spite of the confusion and the bewildering variety. The content of an industrial system must be in some measure determined by local resources—by local minerals, by available fuel, by water, power, and climate. This is particularly the case in the early stages of growth. A typical progression is to begin to work up a raw material hitherto exported in a virgin state. Britain made this switch very early in its industrial history when in the fifteenth century it changed from the export of raw wool to that of woolen textiles. Ghana no longer exports logs but has built up a timber industry to export sawed wood. Oil-producing areas stop exporting crude oil, build their own refineries, and find they can begin to create a chemical industry on the side.

This process is helped when local fuel is not too expensive and when the manufactured export is lighter and more compact and carries less transport costs than in its raw condition. The Volta Scheme in Ghana is designed to bring about such a transformation of Ghana's exports of raw bauxite. Cheap electricity from the Volta Dam would give power to a local smelter, aluminum would be exported and in time no doubt would also be worked up locally into pots and pans and roofing and all aluminum's thousand other uses.

Another typical approach to industrialization is to begin to fabricate locally goods which have hitherto been imported. If there are local skills and local resources, the saving on transport costs gives local industry a competitive advantage. In any case, most governments are prepared to give their industries some protection in the early stages. Tariffs are a perfectly legitimate safeguard for "infant industries." They become harmful only when they bolster the position of permanently high-cost industries or safeguard huge developed markets which need no such protection. It is difficult, for instance, to think of such American giants as General Electric or General Motors as infant industries. Yet sections of their activities are heavily protected.

The successful local production of consumer goods depends, like every other approach to industrialization, upon local power. This need for local fuel explains why, in the past, coal fields have been the origins of most industry to this day. Local supplies of coal and iron ore are the most solid foundation for industrialization. But electricity has opened new doors. Nuclear energy will open more. There are few communities that cannot undertake some transformation of their economies.

The other necessity is an expanding market. The mere presence of a single vast installation—for instance, an oil refinery—does not push a whole community towards industrialization unless other sectors of the economy are being transformed at the same time and new money incomes coming into being which new enterprises can satisfy. This is another reminder of the necessity of a dynamic agriculture with rising productivity at work to boost farm incomes and release workers from the farms. In many parts of Latin America, for instance, a considerable amount of industrial activity has still not drawn the whole community into an upward spiral of development because the countryside remains in the leaden torpor of peonage.

This creation of markets and stimulus to the use of local resources are, of course, not the only methods of initiating the industrial phase. Governments can simply plunge in and do it—setting up factories and power stations and planning a whole industrial setup on the model of Russia's first Five Year Plan. We shall come back to this when we look at the organization of industry. But here one might say that if a government, in planning an industrial structure, gets too far away from the realities of local resources and local power, the industrial structure may be so expensive that in the short run, and perhaps the longer run, too, it tends to lower living standards, not raise them. Since the war, many countries which earlier exported raw materials—Brazil, for instance, or Argentina—have not always been judicious in their industrial plans, and high-cost industry has replaced profitable primary exports. Industry, in short, is not a magic wand. It is perfectly possible to build the wrong factory in the wrong place for the wrong purpose. Incidentally, much of Eastern Europe's forced industrialization under the Communists suffered from these defects. Factories were built for which the raw materials were not available. They remained, deserted hulks of steel and cement, as a monument to the overplanners' zeal.

When we turn to the question of the organization of industry—by private enterprise, by public ownership, by a mixed system—there are two points to remember. The first is that the first great innovations occurred—largely in Britain—as a result of the inventiveness of individual mechanics, investors, and industrialists. The patterns of industry were first established not by government fiat but by a bustling, thriving group of individual men, driven in part by the idea of gain but also by the desire to create.

Once, however, these methods of production were established, they were available as patterns for industrialization anywhere. It is one of the amenities of a world in which communication is possible on so vast a scale that we do not have to invent things twice. If somebody will invent them for us, we can take over the copyright. In fact, since recorded history began, the great mass of mankind has always lived on everybody else.

One of the reasons why all talk of racial superiority or inferiority is so much detestable nonsense is that if you take the whole history of humanity, few groups have lived without borrowing heavily for enlightenment from others. The extent to which, for example, Europe was at one time entirely dependent for all its major inventions upon the peoples of the Middle East is something which Europeans, every now and then, have a habit of forgetting. Yet it is salutary for them to remember that they did not invent the alphabet and that the Phoenicians did. So let us have no nonsense about racial superiority. Mankind possesses and shares a vast patrimony of ideas contributed from a thousand sources. In the great tasks of civilization we are indeed all "members one of another."

The Industrial Revolution was invented in Britain. It has since spread all around the world, and although the basic processes have been repeated—the transfer of wealth from agriculture, the building-up of power resources, the creation of a framework of transportation and urban development, the passing of more and more productive processes from the home to the factory and the machine—the types of organization have varied very greatly; and again and again, when we look at the structure of a particular industrial society, we shall see how deeply its own past history has influenced its industrial shape. This, then, is the second point to keep in mind—the relative continuity of historical experience even through so great an upheaval as the coming of industry.

In the Western world, the tradition of industrialism is in the main one of independent action by many different centers of authority—a pattern with roots in the early development of plural power and individual initiative in Western Europe. This does not mean private activity, pure and unalloyed. Few people would follow Herbert Spencer in demanding that government should get out of the post office and education. Even in the United States, where the gospel of keeping government activity to a minimum is preached with ideological fervor, the percentage of government activity is higher than in India, which proclaims a "socialistic framework." But it remains broadly true that in Western Europe, the Commonwealth nations of European stock, and in North America, the determining factor in the economy is a great variety of industrial enterprises producing for a free market and guided in their policies by the profit motive. And this pattern, however greatly its sophistication has been increased in our own day, also prevailed in the mercantile countries of the Middle Ages, from which so many modern business techniques —of accounting, of banking, of foreign trade—are in fact derived. The Fuggers and the Medicis, bankers of the late Middle Ages, would find their way comfortably around Wall Street or Lombard Street today—in fact, Lombard Street is named after some of them.

Perhaps I should say a word here about the profit motive, since it is the dynamo of the most productive economies the world has ever known. It has acquired so many maleficent overtones and undertones, so intertwined with all the demonology of Marxism, so confounded with the picture of large gentlemen with cigars, top hats, and Astrakhan collars jumping on the inert bodies of the suffering workers that it is hard to disentangle what its economic function is. I suppose one might most simply say, as one businessman has said: "The most important thing about the profit motive is that it is really the avoidance-of-loss motive." In other words, you cannot carry on a business if you do not sell your goods for the amount of money it costs to produce them. This is a fundamental proposition, incidentally, in all industries, including public or state industry, because, in the long run, the fact that you cannot pay out more than you are receiving is a law of nature from which no economy can escape.

In the private sector, the profit motive is the measure by which you estimate that the public is prepared to pay for your goods roughly what it has cost you to produce them. These costs, of course, include much more than the cost of labor, materials, and present and future capital. Profits also cover the strictly entrepreneurial costs—planning for the future, assessing risks, laying in stocks at the right time, and that indefinable quality which gives some men their uncanny sense of what the public wants and how the market will develop. Marxist ideologies were so ludicrously ignorant of the actual management of business that Lenin sincerely believed in 1917 that a carpenter or a cook or a plumber could be taken from the bench and given the direction of a factory. But these are highly skilled functions, and it is from profits that they have to be met.

There are, of course, illegitimate profits—monopoly profits gained by cornering a market and holding consumers up to ransom, profits gained by gross underpayment of a working force which is disorganized or terrorized—but under normal Western conditions, the profit motive has proved a reasonably accurate guide to consumer choice—which is what, in the last analysis, economies exist to satisfy.

But if the dominant system is to be private enterprise, one thing is indispensable—private entrepreneurs. And here, of course, we meet one of the limitations imposed by historical experience. Large parts of Asia and all tribal Africa have not gone through the training in local initiative, in municipal authority and private trade which went together to create the merchant, the banker, and the businessman of early industrialism in the West. At first, in underdeveloped communities, there are no groups of people with entrepreneurial capacity to carry on independently the tasks of production. Least of all is there a whole class eager and waiting to do it—as there had been in Britain. However, once the model of industrial society has come into existence, other countries can copy it by methods which conform to their own historical experience. The Japanese, for instance, had a strong government, strong feudal clans, and a skilled merchant class. The solution they adopted consisted of first establishing industry by government fiat. Then, when the concerns were in running order and younger men had been trained in the business offices of the West, the big enterprises were handed over to the clans and the merchants; their growth stimulated in turn small artisan groups and families to industrialize at the other end of the scale. Government initiative was decisive, but a form of private enterprise followed. In Turkey, too, with its earlier tradition of despotic government, the government itself initiated the industrial program. But dislike of Communism was one factor in ensuring that some government-owned industry was then transferred to private groups.

In India, a sort of halfway house is planned, which once again reflects a profound historic experience. In the nineteenth century, during the British phase of administration, ideas of free enterprise and private management flowed in from the British commercial community; as the century advanced, Indian industry began to develop, particularly in textiles. Yet the secular traditions of India are, as we have seen, bureaucratic. The great enterprises were based upon the state and upon its servants. So it is not surprising that this superimposition of recent upon ancient experience has led India to evolve a mixed economy, with most weight, perhaps, on the public sector but with a place allowed for private development.

In Russia and China we meet the extremes of total governmental control, and this is not entirely a reflection of Communist ideology. The roots go deeper into history. The Chinese have always had a central bureaucracy. As we have seen, the early management of its water power and agriculture required centralized control. The state has always exercised immense influence over the economy, organizing it, directing it, holding monopolies of vital commodities. Private enterprise is connected with the period of national eclipse at the turn of the century when foreign interests had the run of China and Chinese felt dispossessed in their father's house. Chinese Communism has thus drawn not only on ideology but on a profound historical experience.

Even Russia, with its closer links with the West, has always been a predominantly government-directed land. Peter the Great began its forcible modernization and industrialization. In spite of much foreign capital entering the country in the nineteenth century—and thus linking the idea of foreign intervention to "economic enslavement"—the Russian state was the largest employer of labor and the largest landlord in 1914. Once again, the Communists have built upon a bureaucratic, despotic tradition that is infinitely older than they.

Thus, if we look at our present world, we see almost a full spectrum of industrialization, from the predominantly private enterprise of the West through those economies in which public and private activity are mixed in varying degrees, right over to the total planning of the totalitarian states. And much of this spectrum is determined not by ideology but by concrete historical experience. And in future industrialized lands, this is likely still to be the case.

Before we leave the question of industrialism there is one last thing I would like to add. The differences between the various forms and patterns of modern industrial life are, as we have seen, wide enough to make up a complete economic spectrum from free to totally controlled. Yet this variety should not blind us to the fact of how much they also have problems in common. And the greatest problem is the problem that may always haunt mankind; the problem that springs from man always wanting more things than he has material means to provide. In other words, economics is still basically a science concerned with trying to make scarce means cover a great many desirable and incompatible ends. Whether you are a Soviet Commissar, or a Minister of Finance in Ghana, or the Chancellor of the Exchequer, you still have that same problem: what shall we do and what shall we leave out, since our resources do not permit us to do everything?

No economy in the world, for instance, entirely escapes the issue of inflation and deflation. But what are they? In simplest terms, inflation follows when you try to do too much with a given amount of resources, deflation when you do too little. The Communists may have more drastic methods of dealing with these problems—for instance, canceling a whole nation's savings to reduce the inflationary risk. But the problems themselves cannot be exorcised.

What we can say of industrialism is that it has enormously increased man's means. It has, therefore, equally increased his range of choice; it has given him dynamism, it has given him a larger measure of freedom, but it has not yet removed from him all of the elementary economic choices that he has always had to make. In his tremendous advance from primitive agriculture to dynamic industrialization, he has taken some of his old problems along. It is possible, as Lord Keynes once suggested, that future advances in industry and science will free us from the shackles of restricted choice and that art, beauty, the cultivation of the spirit, not economic accumulation, will become the chief purpose of man. Some people argue that America is beginning to approach that point. But mankind as a whole has not yet crossed the threshold of the abundant life. Human life is still one of stern necessity and unavoidable choice.

Chapter Three

Colonialism

WHEN we study colonialism, we are looking at one of the most far-reaching and widespread activities of mankind. It seems to be a fact of human nature that when one group of people becomes more powerful than another group, its instinct is to take over the weaker neighbor.

Like all instincts, it is very old. In fact, it goes to the origins of human organization in tribalism. The early history of tribal society is, to a great extent, a history of conquest, reconquest and conquest again. The rise and fall of empires with which so much of subsequent history has been concerned have their roots in the very

(79)

beginning of man's political activity. When, for instance, the British began to press forward in Nyasaland, they found the local Nyasas under the despotic control of the Yaos, who were busy selling their subordinates to Arab slavers. Or, an example from West Africa: it is as late as 1804 that the Fulani tribe took control by conquest of the Hausa peoples of Northern Nigeria. So it was at the beginning of organized human society and so it has been everywhere, on through time and space until our own day.

One of the most remarkable things about this century is that it is just possible that colonialism, as a recognized principle of political organization, may be on the way out. If so, it will—short of the abolition of war—be the greatest political revolution that mankind has ever seen. Conquest has been man's oldest and most endemic activity. In fact, if we rid ourselves of conquest, we shall have done away with nine-tenths of the causes of war.

However, the results of conquest are by no means the same. One can distinguish many types of imperialism, and there are three broad groups which I should like to examine here. The first is a type of imperialism which brings with it beneficent consequences. For this to happen, a number of conditions must, I think, be fulfilled. One is that the conquering people must have better techniques and a higher degree of civilization than the people they overcome. There is an exception to this that I shall mention, but, broadly speaking, an evolved society has the best chance of practicing beneficent imperialism. A second condition is that in the process of conquest, the conquerors' gifts—the techniques, the culture, the arts and graces, the greater skills in political and economic life—should be fully shared with the conquered people. And a third condition is that out of the conquest—which, in these conditions, amounts to a diffusion of civilization—a new synthesis and a new unity should arise which, in a true sense, is richer and more varied than what went before.

Some colonial imperial systems have, broadly speaking, fulfilled these conditions. Perhaps the most notable example is the Chinese Empire—the longest and most consistent of all imperial patterns. The gradual extension of Chinese dominion from the Yellow River down to the frontiers of Annam went on for about fifteen hundred years, and the Chinese were able, little by little, to extend to all manner of tribal groups and all manner of primitive peoples a much higher way of life in the artistic and intellectual as well as in the material sense. These subject peoples were drawn into the Chinese cultural system and became in time full members of a new all-Chinese civilization.

Another historical example of an empire which, on the whole, was beneficent in its result, can be found in the West. The Roman Empire began in devastation and violence, in the throes and despairs of civil war on an imperial scale, but during its greatest days, it maintained order and peace over a vast area, preserved civilization where it was flickering out, and extended it to tribal peoples still living in a barbarian condition. This it accomplished because, like the Chinese, it allowed the benefits of its civilization to be fully grasped by the people it conquered. The proud boast, "I am a Roman citizen" could be said by men all the way from Britain to Antioch, regardless of their race or previous cultural background. So great was the vision of order left behind by this Roman Empire that for a thousand years after its collapse, the peoples of Europe made attempts—abortive attempts, it is true—to recreate something of the political unity and the scale of civilized communication which had been possible under the Roman Empire.

I would like now to note the exception to the rules of "beneficent imperialism" I have been trying to establish. In general, it is the civilized and developed conqueror who is most likely to turn his conquest into a valuable achievement of cultural and political integration. But there are notable exceptions. It is possible for conquerors, although they are at a lower level of technical and intellectual civilization, to absorb from the people they conquer a higher standard of culture, and bring to it a freshness and a vigor which were lacking in the old and sometimes effete civilization they conquer. When first the Ionian and then the Dorian Greeks entered the old decaying Mycenaean Empire, their new vigor and the old arts combined to create what we must still call the greatest and most dynamic civilization known to man.

Another example—and one most pregnant with consequences for the world today—is the coming of Islam. When the primitive tribal groups of Arabia burst out of the Arabian Peninsula under the leadership of Mohammed and overran the whole of the civilized but stagnant empires of the Persian and the Byzantine monarchies, they absorbed into their new Arabic culture, with its specifically Arabic language, riches of antiquity, of Greek learning, of Christian and Zoroastrian philosophy, scholarship, and art which, as it were, became fertilized by their new energy and by the freshness of their approach. The result was an outburst of cultural achievement along the Mediterranean unequaled until the European Renaissance.

For one last example, we may turn to China. In the seventeenth century, the Chinese imperial government was taken over by the Manchus, a semicivilized people from the North. But Chinese culture inspired the Manchus with such respect that they became more Chinese than the Chinese. In the eighteenth century under such a monarch of genius as Chien Lung, Chinese civilization reached a peak of brilliance and achievement that aroused the wondering admiration of contemporary European philosophers.

But unhappily for our attempts at confident generalization, at this point the example of external conquerors gaining by contact with a superior but conquered civilization breaks down. The very dedication of the Manchus to Chinese Confucian culture was the cause of China's downfall. The new ideas and techniques coming from Europe, with all the force of European expansion behind them, demanded a radical readjustment of old Confucian ideas. But the Manchus, late converts, would not alter one iota of the Confucian classical framework of Chinese society. This refusal deprived China of the power to adapt itself flexibly to the modern world and for nearly a century, the whole empire floundered between dead concepts it could not abandon and living concepts it could not accept. This paralysis, more than anything else, explains why the resurgence of China was delayed until halfway through the middle of this century.

There we will leave these examples of conquests which in one way and another create a new synthesis between conqueror and conquered and turn to a second type of imperialism—an imperialism in which the conquerors did, in fact, bring great gifts of civilization but failed to transfer them thoroughly to the conquered people. Because of this failure no genuine synthesis arose, and there was no real fusion to create a new civilization in which both conqueror and conquered could share.

One example of this, I think, is the impact of the Spanish conquerors on Latin America. The first thing to be said of it is, perhaps, that the Indian population of South America did at least survive. This is not an unimportant point, for, after all, if conquered peoples are to form part of an ultimate synthesis, they must be there to share in it. Some conquered peoples, as we shall see, were not so fortunate. It is, therefore, not a negligible fact that in Latin America the local Indians survived the new forms of society introduced from the West. But to this day it cannot be said that republics with a large Indian population have achieved a genuine synthesis between the more civilized, better-educated groups of Spanish and Portuguese origin, and the great mass of the Indian peasants and mountain people.

There has been a considerable fusion in culture and religion between the old and the new. It is impossible to see some of the churches of Central and South America without feeling how close below the surface of Christianity lie older cults and remnants of a magical past. But on the feudal estates and in the mines, no synthesis occurred. The Indians were the serfs, the peons, the laborers at the bottom of the ladder. The Spanish and Portuguese settlers were carried on their backs. One of the causes of political instability in much of Latin America in the last century has been the stirring revolt of the Indian masses against the old European domination; another, the emergence of new leadership. Because of this, we should perhaps say that the story is not yet finished. In the colonial period proper, before the Latin American republics threw off their direct links with the Iberian peninsula, no true synthesis emerged. But the ferment has gone on working. It is perhaps only in the next century that we shall see in final form an Indian-European civilization based upon a full integration of both cultural traditions.

It is probably true to say that most conquests have been of this type. The conquerors often brought superior techniques and more advanced ways of living. They opened up new possibilities and even ended periods of stagnation. But they remained to exploit and to rule. They failed to integrate themselves with the local peoples and after a certain period, their alienness, their failure to intermarry, to settle, to produce a new joint class of leaders and governors caused their subjects to overlook any of the coincident advantages of their rule and to think of one thing only—how to be rid of them. We shall come back to this point when we look at the modern colonial record.

Before we consider the third category of conquest— the wholly evil destructive conquests that darken the record of humanity—we should look at one kind of "colonialism" which fits very uneasily into any of our categories. From one point of view, it is highly destructive. From another, it has led to the creation of tremendously powerful and civilized societies. As a type of conquest, it lies somewhere between our categories, in a contradictory class of its own.

There are cases in history where the gap between the civilization of the conquerors and the social organization of the conquered is so vast that it seems no bridge is possible between them. I have in mind here, for example, the settlements made by British migrants in Australia. There they found a small, scattered, local population living as the Bushmen live in Central Africa. These Australian aborigines had hardly even achieved primitive tribal organization or institutions. They did not practice agriculture in any form. They belonged, in short, to the very first stages of man's ascent up the ladder of civilized humanity. It was now their tragic fate to be faced with men and women living at the other end of the scale—in the increasingly complex, scientific, industrialized society of the nineteenth and twentieth centuries.

Modern industrial civilization, with its technical evolution and intellectual drive, is, as we know, the most aggressive form of civilization that mankind has ever known. Its twin impact of science and industry is one that involves a total transformation of all aspects of life—not only of organization and technique but of fundamental habits of thought and social behavior. You have only to consider the impact of this type of society upon people who have not yet moved beyond the simplest patterns of living and working to see that, without immense patience, understanding, and restraint, the incoming settlers will annihilate the whole social apparatus of the backward local peoples. Yet these qualities are not usually the qualities of conquerors or pioneers.

The usual result is that the conquered groups can find no place in the new form of society and live on as miserable scattered remnants in isolated reserves. One cannot say that the newcomers intended these results in a cold-blooded, methodical way. Yet their actual behavior has led to some of the most heartbreaking human tragedies that can occur, for no one is more defenseless than primitive man, snatched from his traditional security and plunged into the ruthless, dynamic society of the modern West.

The same process was at work in the settlement of the United States. The original Red Indian tribes were hunters and food-gatherers. They had not yet achieved settled agriculture. Of all ways of life, nomadic existence fits most unreadily into the advancing pattern of modern agriculture and industrialization. The men and women of European stock settling on the North American continent steadily increased the range, power, and complexity of their society. The Indians fought a long rearguard action against this advance but could not adapt themselves to it in any way. Once again, the gap in culture was too great for a synthesis to occur, and in the end, the local peoples were brought to total and pitiable stagnation.

Yet one cannot dismiss the settlers' achievements as negative and destructive. The society they built has since opened its doors to millions of men and women of different stock and nationality and created a community whose people have a better chance to live a life based upon free choice and human respect than in any other age or clime.

Nor should one suggest for a moment that the problems created by the gap in culture are confined to areas of European settlement. All Asia has records of local tribes totally submerged by incoming peoples of higher culture. These problems belong not to our color, but to our humanity. To give only one instance, the aboriginal inhabitants of Japan may have been of white, or as some people like to call it, Aryan stock. Their way of life was too primitive to stand up to the higher techniques and greater culture of the Japanese, and today the "hairy Ainu" is a scattered, miserable remnant on one of the northern islands—a salutary lesson, no doubt, to white racial supremacists, but a tragic example once again of what can occur in the encounter between local primitive people and the expansive force of conquerors of a higher civilization and technique.

One last group of imperialisms must be mentioned— the utterly malign and destructive empires of which, unhappily, there are one or two in the human record. Of the Assyrians, it is known in general only that "they came down like a wolf on the fold." But, unlike so many oddments of folklore, this piece of information is by no means irrelevant, because this is exactly what they did. In the records of antiquity, the activities of the Assyrian people read like a death-knell. They swept down from the north to the great river valleys of Mesopotamia and the "fertile crescent" of the Levant—the most highly civilized areas in the Middle East—and there destroyed kingdoms and principalities, butchered the people and razed the cities, and finally extinguished themselves in a perpetual cycle of aggressive war.

This last point is worth noting. It seems to me that one of the great arguments for the ultimate moral governance of the universe—and hence for the future hopes of mankind—is that pure aggression and undiluted destructiveness are entirely barren. Sometimes, when we look at the long chronicle of history and "consider the injustices that are done under the sun," the hopes betrayed, the sorrows without cure, we may feel that the whole record is a senseless tangle of violence and outrage and despair. Yet evil does not survive if it is wholly evil. The end of a monster like Hitler is there to remind us that, beyond a certain point, violence and evil are self-liquidating. Indeed, nowhere is the utter sterility of pure violence more obvious than in the life cycle of what may well be the most totally destructive empire in all history.

From the beginning of the thirteenth century, for about two hundred years, the great civilized areas of mankind, in China, in India, in Persia, in the Middle East, in Russia were at the mercy of the most bloodthirsty marauders known to man—the Mongol riders of the steppe. The name of Genghis Khan is remembered for little but butchery and destruction. When his horsemen came to Baghdad, then at the height of the glory of the Abbasid Caliphate, what did they do? They razed the city, they burned an irreplaceable library of priceless books, and they left a pyramid of half a million skulls in the main square. North India was sacked and China spared only because the great Khan was persuaded to believe that the Chinese would be more useful working than dead. Such was the scale of this appalling outbreak of primitive destructiveness.

But now comes the pregnant postscript. The Mongols left no creative tidemarks on the shores of history. Their imperial control came and vanished again as quickly as their raiding hordes. They themselves quarreled over their heritage, and within three centuries of their eruption, virtually nothing remained—no culture with a Mongol stamp, no dynasty, no lasting achievement of any sort. Thus, once again, the final victim of the total tyrant is shown to be the tyrant himself. There have been wholly maleficent empires, but by that very fact they do not last.

II

Now with these very broad generalizations about the nature of empire in mind, let us look at some of the imperial problems of our own day. We may, I think, begin with an imperial record of which the last chapter is being written. Save for a few tiny outposts such as Hong Kong or Macao, nothing survives of the Western imperial system in Asia. In the last ten or eleven years, a whole phase of human history has been concluded. European colonization of Asia has come to an end. How, then, should we judge it according to the criteria that we have established for beneficent—and less beneficent—empires? How does the record look, now that we are beginning to see it in perspective?

There are three points to consider: the character and quality of the conquerors, the extent to which they brought benefits to the conquered, and the question whether some sort of final synthesis was worked out between them. This last point, I admit, is difficult to establish, for we are dealing with a system which only came to an end the day before yesterday. The synthesis could, conceivably, lie in the future. Certainly, on the analogy of earlier empires, the 150 years the British spent in India is a very short time for any sort of genuine cultural fusion to be achieved. But judgments will be passed, nonetheless, for in the twentieth century we live with a markedly accelerated view of time. We expect everybody to be civilized in ten years, whereas the Chinese went on civilizing for over fifteen hundred. The revolutionary changes in our spatial relationships have been matched by a speeding-up in our time cycle and in our temporal relationships as well. The difficult we do today, the impossible tomorrow. Given this estimate of time's efficacy, the European record can already be judged.

Since there is not space here to follow the activities of all the European colonizers, I shall refer in the main to the British, whose activities were in any case the most sustained and widespread. The first point to discuss is whether as colonizers they brought to Asia superior gifts and techniques and thus helped to raise and enhance local standards. And we run into a difficulty here right away, for the British conquerors changed enormously in the course of their conquests. When the first British traders came out to Asia, they were very far from superior in technical civilization to the people with whom they now came into contact. As we have already seen, the civilizations of Asia at the turn of the seventeenth century were in many artistic and cultural values superior to the culture of Europe. When in the eighteenth century, the British King, George III, sent Lord Macartney to ask the great Manchu Emperor, Chien Lung, to open trade relations with Britain, the Emperor replied: "The Celestial Empire possesses all things in prolific abundance and lacks no product within its borders. There is therefore no need to import the manufactures of outside barbarians in exchange for our own products." He added that he was nevertheless gratified that the British King "dwelling at the ends of the sea" had shown his readiness to pay homage to the supreme Emperor and was graciously willing to send back some gifts in return.

Such was the opinion of the Chinese Emperor in the eighteenth century of the British merchants who wanted to come out and establish themselves as traders in his territory. Nor at that time was Chien Lung's estimate of what the West had to offer too wide of the mark. One of the reasons for the disgraceful development of British sales of opium to China at the turn of the eighteenth century was that it offered the only alternative to paying good bullion for silks and porcelains European

(93)

markets were pressing to buy.

But in the late eighteenth century, the Europeans began to become much more formidable. Under the drive of forces we have already described—free institutions, scientific discoveries and the coming of the Industrial Revolution—a complete change occurred in the balance of power. The new techniques made these tiny bodies of Europeans more formidable than anything that Asia had seen since the Mongol raiders. In a sense, this change of balance does not strictly determine whether the incoming Europeans were now more highly civilized than the Asian lands. In ceremonies and public monuments, in gardens and temples, in beauty, philosophical riches, and length of tradition, Asia was still a supremely cultivated place.

But in the nineteenth and twentieth century, the values that were coming to the fore were hard, driving, rational, scientific values, the application of mind to the material substratum of existence in order to make it work and produce, the manipulation and creation of new machines, a scientific curiosity about all causes and effects; and with this went a drive to national consciousness and political self-expression new in the history of mankind.

With this equipment, the European impact was that of a battering-ram when it reached Asia, knocking the breath out of venerable tradition and shattering any institution of which the foundations were already flawed. It was as though a hurricane had struck the

East, and to a very considerable extent the authors of this hurricane knew as little of what they were doing as the winds themselves.

They say that the British Empire was acquired in a fit of absence of mind. There is an element of truth here, in that the Westerners went out to Asia not to conquer but to trade. Wherever local conditions were stable enough and local authority powerful enough to maintain order, no conquest occurred. Japan, as we have seen, simply excluded all merchants once the Shoguns realized the unsettling effect of the European traders and missionaries. China had enough of a central government even in the decadence of the Manchus to prevent outright colonization. But the petty warring principalities of South East Asia and Indonesia were no match for the vigor of the incoming traders bent on concessions and monopolies and always ready to take a hand in dynastic politics, backing the more compliant Sultan against his rivals and thus taking all effective power out of his hands.

The most momentous instance of local weakness inviting foreign intervention occurred, however, in India itself. Had the Mogul Empire survived to the nineteenth century, it is safe to say there would have been no British Empire in India. But when the British traders began to arrive and began the process of protecting their position against other—mainly French—trading rivals, the Mogul Empire was in dissolution. Local princes fought for the succession and the foreign traders joined in the fights, playing one pretender off against another. In the disorders, British power steadily grew as it took responsibility for stable local conditions— stable for trade, I need hardly say. This was not a planned, stage-by-stage effort of conquest but a largely spontaneous response to the collapse of local authority.

Now, I do not say that ambitious Britons on the spot did not accelerate the process. In fact, a useful monograph could be written about the consequences for Asia of the late development of the telegraph system. In the 1860's, for instance, an active young British Army Lieutenant, fighting the Taiping rebellion in the Yangtse valley of China, proposed to annex the valley to Britain. He cabled to London saying in effect: "Can easily annex the whole of the Yangtse basin. Do you want it?" Back came a horrified cable from London on the theme: "Down, Sir! Down, Sir! Put it down!"

I often think that if, in the earlier phases of the occupation of India, men like Lord Wellesley had been obliged to cable: "Would you like me to take over the rest of Bengal?" the expansion of British power in India might have taken a very different course. But since it took six months to get an answer from London, the men on the spot had a freedom which disappeared once the telegraph took over. This fact underlines how little the British conquerors of India were working to a plan of expansion laid down in advance by the central government at home.

However, even if they were inadvertent colonizers,

colonizers they remain. How did they acquit themselves? Having come into their colonial heritage partly by way of trade, what did they do with it? Were the consequences beneficent or baleful? To what category of empire-builders should they be assigned?

Perhaps the best way to illustrate the strength and the weakness of the system is to return to the comparison made on an earlier page—between the differing fates of India, China, and Japan under the Western impact. As we have seen, their experience provides a sort of spectrum of the whole Asian experience—India completely absorbed into a western empire, China battered and shaken and torn, the direct responsibility of no one, barely even of its own government, and Japan resisting the Western onslaught completely until it was ready after 1870 to modernize itself and initiate the process of industrialization in its own way and under its own leadership. Each case illustrates some aspect of Western colonialism, the good and the bad.

Let us begin with India. By taking over the administration of the subcontinent, the British became responsible for the whole society—directly in British India, indirectly but effectively in the princely states. In many ways, this responsibility was exercised soberly and justly. The British restored the old boast of the Indian Imperial tradition—of the Mauryas and Guptas and Moguls in their greatest days—that a woman could safely walk alone with a bag of gold on her head from one end of the realm to the other. "Law and order" is a condition we take for granted until we lose it. Its restoration and maintenance in India for over a hundred years was an incalculable blessing—especially for the peasant—after the violent foundering of the Moguls.

"Law and order" allowed the population to surge ahead. British responsibility had to extend to the feeding of the masses and the prevention of famine. A modern network of railways in India was set up not only to assist trade but also to ensure the movement of food from surplus to deficit areas. Vast irrigation schemes were launched to bring more land under grain. In fact, when India became independent, it had more irrigated land than any other ten countries put together. In a wide variety of ways, modern techniques and methods were introduced over the years and economic growth enjoyed the background which it most requires —that of security and legality. All these are not negligible benefits. And they were reinforced by something of even greater significance.

If you believe—as I do—that the most valuable and yet most precarious human good is freedom, the British imperialists must be allowed their part in bringing this great ferment to the East. Concepts of self-government and individual rights were no part of the Asian tradition. There had been wise governments and benevolent governments and magnificent governments—but never one that was free. In retrospect the British may be proud of having helped to create in India the attitudes of mind, the temper and the philosophy which were among the forces which ultimately drove them out.

They may not have been great educators in the sense of creating a modern mass educational system. How would they do it in India when as late as 1870 they had not done so at home? The government was essentially a "law and order" government, not a modernizing one. But British rule was not obscurantist either. Most of the time, the inflow of new ideas was encouraged, not banned. Indians who wished could obtain British education. Schools were opened in India by public and missionary bodies. It was still education of an elite, but it was in the new, liberal tradition.

You may be inclined to question the paradox that imperialism can bring freedom. But the British who came to India to trade and stayed to govern could not leave all their ideas and philosophies at home. In the 1820's, men of the stamp of Munro and Elphinstone already spoke of the duty to train Indians for self-government and saw it as the only justification of the British presence. It was an English official, Alan Hume, who first founded the Indian National Congress to arouse interest among Indians in the tasks of government. The British brought the ferment whether they liked it or not—and some of them did not—and as the decades passed and popular rights became steadily more assured in Britain, the ferment strengthened and spread in India—the ferment of men who believed they should enjoy the rights of liberal government, and that among those inalienable rights was that of not being ruled by anyone else.

This concept, as I have said before, I believe to be a new departure in the history of mankind. There have been many revolts against conquerors in the past but I think it is only in the nineteenth and twentieth century that we have started to formulate, within a recognized international code, the principle that nations have the inherent right not to be part of other peoples' empires. And this, as we have seen, is fundamentally a projection of the Western development of political rights within the national community. And it was the West that carried it round the world.

But the Europeans came primarily to trade, and many of the evils which are now remembered against them spring from the single-mindedness with which they set about making the most of their economic opportunities. Sometimes the mischief was direct, conscienceless exploitation. There were famines in Java in the mid-nineteenth century because peasants had been compelled to grow export crops to the neglect of foodstuffs.

Sometimes it sprang from economic developments which simply bypassed the local inhabitants. At the turn of the nineteenth century, there were fantastic developments in raw-material production in South East Asia. Between 1880 and 1914 the swamps of the lower Irrawaddy were transformed into one of the greatest rice-producing areas of the world. Malaya became the greatest supplier of tin and rubber. But in Burma only

European merchants and Indian middlemen took the profit. The Burmese peasant ended, as often as not, bankrupt and expropriated as well. In Malaya, Europeans and Chinese were the organizers—and absorbers —of the new wealth. It was not surprising that the Malayans accepted Japanese conquest so passively, nor that the first act of the independent Burmese government in 1947 was to nationalize practically everything —in order, primarily, to take the nation's entire resources out of foreign hands. Second thoughts have, incidentally, modified this policy.

Perhaps the most damaging and pervasive economic disturbances sprang not from direct exploitation but from the unplanned consequences of the European incursion. In the earlier Asian economies a rough balance existed in the village between farming and handicrafts. The local products eked out farm income, helped to build a merchant class in the city and had already led in some areas to the development of large-scale production—of calico from Calcutta, for instance, or muslins from Dacca, and all the range of silks and porcelains from China shipped out through Canton. These workshops and handicraft centers would have been— as they were later in Japan—one of the bases of future industrialization and modernization.

But it was this whole structure that was shattered by the flooding-in of European manufactures in the nineteenth century. One can see the full effect of this economic tornado in China. The old handicrafts were destroyed, ruin in the villages deepened; the government had not the power or capacity to resist the foreign traders and investors. They set up factories in free ports wrested from the Emperor, and industrialization began not in the country at large under local auspices—as in Britain—but in the treaty ports under foreign ownership. In time, some Chinese joined in and even became very wealthy. But behind them, the vast moribund countryside sank into an ever-deepening crisis of peasant debt and despair.

India suffered less heavily, for it had a working administration, and while the British certainly did not encourage local industrialization—they were free-trade men, and Lancashire did not like the idea of Indian tariffs against British cotton goods—they did not forbid it, and their orderly administration provided a stable background for experiment. The manufacture of local textiles grew strongly and the energetic Tata family even contrived in the face of British discouragement to lay the foundations of an iron and steel industry. As in so many other countries, the two world wars also accelerated and diversified India's nascent industrialization.

But how far all this is from anything we could recognize as a policy of national development can be seen —as I have suggested—by comparing the experience of China and India with that of Japan. First by rigorously excluding the Westerners and then by adapting their system in a vast internal national effort, the Japanese were the first to transform their society and meet the West on its own terms. It is only now, seven or eight decades later, that the Indians and Chinese, in their different fashion, are attempting the formidable task of modernization. In other words, the nation with the least colonial contacts was able to learn most quickly the colonialists' techniques.

Out of this confusing web of good and evil, can we say that something good and lasting has been conserved? Has some synthesis of conquerors and conquered come about? Can we give a verdict yet? One type of synthesis—a warm, local social fusion of two ways of life—was excluded by Western prejudices of color. Since, however, the conquerors in Asia were not permanent settlers, these barriers of color did not become a permanent irritant and in any case are giving ground today.

But at the political level, the readiness of Britain's Asian dominions—with the exception of Burma—to remain in the informal partnership of the Commonwealth suggests that in the balance more weal than ill came from the colonial years and that a working association on the basis of equality between Asia and the West may be more than a Utopian idea. If over the years this association continues and becomes more confident and varied, the synthesis it offers could be fruitful indeed for the human race. There is no skill the nations need to learn more speedily than that of living and working together, and it is hard to exaggerate the importance of any practical working model which shows them how.

III

We come now to the only two large colonial systems left in the world—European colonialism in Africa and Russian colonialism in Europe and possibly in parts of Asia, although, as I have already suggested, the Asian aspect is somewhat more problematical. What shall we say of contemporary imperialism in the light of our criteria—the degree of civilization which the conquerors bring with them, their readiness to share it with the people they conquer and the lasting result for both conquered and conqueror?

One should say, at once, that there can be no single verdict on the whole of Africa. Too many different peoples, too many different policies are involved. But since some generalization is unavoidable, I would say that, broadly speaking, we can distinguish three different approaches to African colonization.

In many areas of Africa, the Europeans came, as they came to Asia, as traders and they stayed for many of the same reasons: the opening up of promising lines of export, the collapse of local authority under their pressure, intense rivalries to keep each other out. And just as the beginning of colonialism in Africa resembled the Asian episode, so, too, does its course and its outcome. I believe such areas as West Africa, parts of East Africa, and the Congo have gained greatly from "law and order"—from the ending of tribal wars, from new concepts of political freedom and the rule of law and from the beginnings, particularly in West Africa, of systematic modern education. In the economic field, the pattern, too, for a considerable time resembled the Asian experience. The traders pursued their own profitable trading, mining, and plantation interests, but they felt no responsibility for development over and above what they needed for themselves. Yet, as in Asia, there were incidental local advantages—ports built, roads extended, public utilities introduced—and local people with sufficient initiative could play some part in the new market economy that was being built on the margins of traditional subsistence agriculture.

Moreover, since the last war, the old *laisser faire* economics have been modified. A new sense of responsibility for colonial peoples has taken its place. Grants from welfare and development funds, schemes for accelerated education, a new interest in native agriculture—these represented a new approach which, in some areas, has amounted to little less than a revolution. In French Africa, before and after independence, The French Government has spent about $300 million a year in Direct Grants. These territories, together with the former Belgian colony of Congo, have also benefited by a Common Market Fund of over $1000 million in the decade after 1958. British grants have averaged about $70 million a year.

In short, the African experience in some areas has

been more generous and constructive than the earlier Asian model. There has been more direct effort to assist local peoples and less reliance upon the beneficial side-effects of pursuing metropolitan interests. There is therefore a strong likelihood that parts of Africa will follow the Indian model in their post-colonial associations. Ghana, like India, has decided to remain an equal, independent partner in the Commonwealth. The territories formerly attached to the countries of the Common Market have formed a well articulated association with it and with each other. Only in the Portuguese areas does the future road seem barred. It is perhaps a safe generalization to make that throughout most of the African lands that lie between the Sahara and the frontiers of the Rhodesias, independence in friendly association with Europe is a possible development of the colonial phase. If this proves the case, there could be no better basis for a lasting, fruitful partnership.

But this, unhappily, is not the only African pattern. In the Union of South Africa, where extensive white settlement—not to speak of Asian settlement—has produced a plural society, there is no hopeful prospect such as I have described. One may admit all the difficulties. The white settlers have been in great measure the organizers and producers of wealth—just as the Chinese have been in Malaya. One can recall the difficulties raised in all mixed communities—Asian or African or European—by the rule of "one man, one vote," which automatically gives political power to the racial majority which may, from the accidents of history, be the least prepared for political responsibility. All this can be admitted. Yet it still remains true that no human community in our day can be founded upon a total contradiction and this, surely, is the present basis of South African policy.

In the Union today, the processes of economic growth are going forward at breakneck speed. With an annual investment of over twenty percent of national income, South Africa has been expanding and diversifying its economy in every direction, even though gold, diamonds, and uranium remain a basic source of wealth. But manufacturing industry has caught up with mining in importance to the national economy.

But all this wealth depends upon the labor of millions of Africans. The 300,000-odd migrant laborers in the gold mines are not the only essential sector of the working force. All the bounding growth of secondary industry depends upon African labor and upon increasingly skilled African labor, too. Yet the political basis of the society is to deny the African any responsible part in a community wholly dependent upon his labors. I do not think that any system based upon so profound a contradiction can endure. Nor, clearly, can there be any hope of reconciliation or cooperation between the various communities. What seems to lie ahead today is not synthesis but explosion.

But the Union is not the only area of mixed migration, where African and Asian and European live side by side. In the Central African Federation of Northern and Southern Rhodesia and Nyasaland, and in Kenya, Europeans have come not only to trade and to organize development but to settle and make their homes. The fateful question in these areas is whether the South African model is to be followed or other more hopeful patterns can be evolved.

In theory, at least, these mixed societies are dedicated to the ideal of equal partnership in a plural society. In practice, they face a difficulty which we have met before—the obstacles to cooperation that exist inevitably when one group of people in a society belongs to a totally different level of cultural and economic development from the others. Sometimes, as in America and Australia, the gap proved too great to be bridged. Moreover, the philosophy of the day did not lay upon the dominant people the duty to do all in their power to bridge the gap. It is possible that, if Central and East Africa had been colonized a century sooner, the tribal Africans might have been reduced to as miserable a remnant as the Hottentots in South Africa.

But in the late nineteenth century, the world's conscience was more alert. King Leopold's decimation of the Congo Africans, for instance, became an international scandal and the Belgian government had to reverse his policy of total exploitation. The Africans thus survived, but still in a primitive, tribal condition. The question for this century is, therefore, still how to bridge the gap.

(108)

This problem, I hasten to add, has nothing to do with racial superiority or inferiority. It has a great deal to do with the stage in the human journey a particular group has reached. In Central Africa, tribal society, much disrupted by local war and by Arab slave raiding, had to meet head-on the new, technical, scientific, rational European thrust from outside. It is hard to exaggerate the gulf of ages between inhabitants of static, traditional, tribal society and the restless, adventurous, individualist Europeans who came in as prospectors and fortune-hunters or the modern commercial and financial organizations which followed in their wake to consolidate and exploit their discoveries. On the one hand, you had small tribal groups still living in the dream world of magic and myth, following their own traditions by instinct and custom; on the other, the twentieth-century techniques, the high-power pressures of materialism, rationalism, gadgetry, and mechanization. Between the modern office buildings shining with chromium, the modern smelters, the vast machines, and the thatched huts out in the native reserves, lie millennia of change and experience. Can millennia be rolled away in a few decades?

Perhaps the first thing to say—since so many people deny it—is that there is nothing inherently impossible in the aim of producing a multiracial society on the basis of partnership and political equality. In the West Indies, for instance, people of divers racial origin have come to form coherent political communities which govern themselves on the basis of full and equal political association. With the development of education, with the passage of time, a new and hopeful synthesis is beginning to emerge in the Caribbean. There is, therefore, no inconceivability about a similar evolution in the communities of mixed racial stock in Africa.

But the West Indies had time. Through three hundred years of stress and trouble and evolutionary changes the new patterns have been worked out not under the fierce light of modern worldwide pressure and publicity but in a local, leisurely way. Nothing of that sort is possible in modern Africa. The whole world's political and racial nerve-ends are far too sensitive for any local policies to remain unnoticed. In any case, to the north, in West Africa the victories of African nationalism are putting the clock forward every hour. If the aim is partnership in a multiracial society, it must be pursued not as a remote "far off, divine event" but as an urgent priority of present policy.

I should like to underline three fundamental conditions of advance. The first is continued economic development, because education, which is the only quick bridge across the millennia, is an expensive business. In Central Africa, so long as the price of copper recovers, the means of development exist. In fact, in few places in the free world has the economy grown at such a rapid pace.

But means alone will not ensure success. They must be deployed in serious, ambitious schemes for general

(110)

education—schemes which really open the door of the future to all citizens, independent of their race or origin. Education has to become the driving, central force of government policy, the goal for which all other amenities are, if necessary, set aside. Cecil Rhodes once claimed his ambition to be: "Equal rights to all civilized men." But the ideal is a mockery unless every energy is bent upon extending civilization—by the only route, education—to the whole body of citizens.

Education, undertaken with this energy, creates the third condition—which is hope. No one pretends that the African in his reserve today can undertake the full direction of a modern community. His fear is that no one of his race, whatever his talents, will ever be allowed to do so. To this fear, massive education is the answer, with no bar set to the capacity of rising young men, black, brown, or white.

Education, too, can offer a rational approach to the inflamed issue of the franchise. To link the vote to educational qualifications is not arbitrary—as are all distinctions based upon race—and it ensures that with each generation leaving school, the aim of "one man, one vote" will be more clearly realized and upon a sound basis of knowledge and responsibility. Today, the obvious degree to which policies in Central Africa fall short of these conditions is a measure of the dangers to peaceful evolution that lie ahead.

Africa is thus a picture of paradox. In Africa South of the Sahara the colonial period plunged a slumbering

continent into the strenuous risks and opportunities of
the twentieth century. In most lands, the passing of
colonial control leaves open the possibility of future
cooperation between men of European and African
stock. But where the Europeans are permanent settlers,
that possibility is either denied—as in South Africa—
or it is in jeopardy. In these areas, the risk is clear that
the legacy of colonialism will not be a new synthesis
but a perpetuation of struggle and hate.

IV

We come now to the question of Russia's empire. I
have already suggested the reasons, on grounds of nationalism, for supposing that Soviet control in Eastern
Europe is unlikely to prove permanent. Here I would
like to add another factor—the inefficacy of Marxism
as an ideological cement to take nationalism's place.

The history of mankind's visions and beliefs suggests
that no political doctrine lasts indefinitely; any very
rigid political doctrine is fortunate if it endures a hundred years. Principles last: the principles of freedom,
for instance, or of self-determination, or of the rule of
law; but immensely complicated theories of human behavior which try to cover everything from mathematics
to market-gardening very rarely survive because, as we
know from human experience, life does not fall into
such neat and preordained patterns. Nor is there anything more ultimately tedious than a vast apparatus
of solemn nonsense designed to explain everything
about everything.

In America recently I met some of the fighters-for-freedom from Budapest. They were among the young students whose protests had set the whole October revolt in motion. Yet they told me that they had not intended to start a revolution. "Do you know what we really wanted?" they said. "We wanted to get rid of the hours of compulsory Marxist indoctrination in our classes." In other words, a whole new generation who were supposed to be the vanguard of the new Communism were so bored that they would rather risk being shot than continue to study it.

Nor do I think that startling new industrial advances in Eastern Europe—of which the foundations are being laid now—will be enough to counteract the spirit of nationalism. On the contrary, the reverse has been true in Europe. The more technically developed a nation becomes, the more its industry and wealth expand, the more conscious it becomes of its own national substance, the less ready to be run by somebody else. It is, therefore, at least possible that the whole process of increasing and encouraging economic growth in Eastern Europe will at the same time increase the tendency of the people to reclaim that national freedom which, historically, they have already enjoyed.

The picture in Soviet Asia is, I think, different. It is not only that many of the Turkish-speaking peoples of Central Asia had little tradition of separate nationhood before they were absorbed by the Czars into the Russian Empire. It is not only that the Soviet leaders by encouraging local tongues and local cultures have avoided a direct and extreme collision with national feeling. The fundamental reason why this vast area of Soviet Asia has the chance of being absorbed into a single massive community—one only less vast than that of China —is that the Communists have fulfilled the conditions which, as I have already suggested, alone make possible the transit from colonial status to a harmonious plural society. These conditions are development, education, and hope.

Even if Soviet figures contain some exaggerations, the scale of industrialization is impressive. Khrushchev claimed in his Report to the Twentieth Party Congress that, compared with 1913, Tadzhik industry had increased twenty-four times, Khirghiz industry thirty-three times and the boom area of Kazakhstan thirty-seven times. In the process, primitive tribesmen have no doubt been herded into towns and factories with as much bewilderment and misery as many of the detribalized migrant workers of Africa. But the survivors are rooted in their new environment and—this is the essential point—their labors are in part devoted directly to their own advance, in other words to a massive effort of education.

Save among elderly people, there is no more illiteracy in Soviet Asia. Republics such as Uzbekistan may spend up to sixty-five percent of their local budget on education; Uzbekistan has today more graduates in proportion to population than France. The major cities are university centers with thousands of students where before 1914 there might have been not a single soul with a university degree. Not all the students are of local origin. Great Russians have streamed in as technicians and settlers. Minority groups from all over Russia have been exiled to these remote regions. Thirty-four different nationalities are represented in Alma-Ata university. But no group is barred by race or nationality. The local people do not have to wait their turn while Great Russian migrants are served first.

And so there is hope—hope of education, of advancement, of work commensurate to talent. And there is no color bar. This does not mean that the political and economic direction of these areas does not remain firmly in Great Russian hands. Nor does it mean that Kazakhs and Uzbeks, Kalmucks and Turks enjoy any kind of political freedom. But they share their servitude on reasonably equal terms with all the other nationalities of Russia and can feel that, if their talents permit, they will one day play a role on the all-Russian stage. The Great Russians, as conquerors and colonizers in Central Asia, may therefore achieve a lasting synthesis of rulers and ruled.

This prospect does not solve the fundamental Soviet dilemma—how to grant freedom and elbowroom as education and well-being advance. But it does mean that no extra disability of birth will hold back the Soviet Union's non-Russian subjects while all Russia's peoples search for the solution.

Chapter Four

Communism

To UNDERSTAND the modern impact of Communism we have to take up again some of the facts that have been outlined on earlier pages. One is the process by which enough capital was saved to set the industrial revolution in motion, another the effect of that revolution when it spread beyond the Atlantic Ocean to embrace all the peoples of mankind. In both cases, as we have seen, the process involved much that was brutal, haphazard, and catastrophic; to these upheavals Communism is the response, brutal in its turn, catastrophic too, and—for all its claim to have deciphered the "objective" laws of history—in very large measure equally haphazard and blind.

The capital—or saving—which launched the new system was provided in part by the men and women who already possessed some wealth—traders, bankers, landowners, artisans with a little money put by. They put these savings in promising undertakings—or lost them in mistakes and bankruptcies. Where the new technique proved successful, they remained sharers in the new wealth and part-owners of the new means of production.

But the great bulk of the saving was provided—as in all subsequent industrial revolutions—by the workers themselves, by the men streaming in from farms and fields to the new cities, working inhumanly long hours for wages that barely kept them and their families alive. The wealth which their efforts created was the source of further investment and of a wider expansion in the power to produce still more goods. Yet in the first decades of industrialism, the workers saw precious little of the new wealth. It enriched the owners and was reinvested by them, but the mass of the people—the laborers working a seventy-hour week, the children of five and six sitting at the looms, or the women who crawled underground, half naked, dragging coal baskets —slaved on in unrelieved conditions of urban squalor.

Today, when we read of the conditions revealed in official Blue Books or described with wrathful realism in such novels as Dickens' *Bleak House* and *Hard Times*, we wonder how such things were allowed to come to pass or, once known, to continue unreformed. Were there no men of conscience? Was it not supposedly a Christian country? Yet every day crimes that in the great tradition of the Bible call to heaven for vengeance —oppressing the poor and defrauding the laborer of his hire—were not simply tolerated. They were in some degree the basis of the system.

The reason was not all wickedness and avarice and greed—although, as in any human order, these played their part. We have to remember the degree to which the whole new process of industrialism was highly mysterious to contemporary thought. Men were not clear how it had started and gathered momentum. There had been no master plan. On the contrary, the origins had lain in a series of independent efforts by entrepreneurs and capitalists, all in a sense working in the dark. They were pursuing profits—that they could see—but they were not consciously taking part in a vast economic and industrial revolution. This was occurring all around them without design or direction and when you consider how strange the new techniques were, how widespread the social upheaval that they brought about, it is not surprising that many people gave the new system the almost magical respect we give to things which seem wholly mysterious.

There was, of course, a rationalization of the mystery. In the eighteenth century the idea had been popular that the Creator had set the whole universe to work as a clockmaker sets a clock. Thus men's instincts, implanted by Nature, were bound to be in tune with Nature's general plan. To pursue one's own interests could not, on this theory, contradict the public weal. On the contrary, private profit equaled public good.

From this, it was an easy step to argue that the "hidden hand" which held all in harmony could be interfered with only at peril to the whole system. To check it or restrain it or divert it might pull out the mainspring and risk the running down of the entire industrial experiment.

This ignorance helps to explain an attitude towards government intervention which seems fantastic to us now. The idea was almost universal that if the government extended its functions beyond those of preserving law and order, it might, in some catastrophic way, bring the whole new, precarious industrial system to collapse. Men of good will, honor, and integrity such as Richard Cobden and John Bright of England were prepared to argue with almost religious fervor that you could not intervene in the economy without ruining it. Even attempts to regulate the hours of work in factories or to stop little children from going into factories and mines would, in some way, impair the harmony of the system and lead, therefore, to the collapse of the whole economy.

Here, then, was a fearsome combination. Change of a revolutionary order was thrust forward by men who were very largely ignorant of the full consequences of what they were doing and at a time when attempts to introduce measures of rational control were regarded as more menacing than the obvious evils they were designed to remove.

In any circumstances, these conditions would have created outrage and protest. And indeed they did. In England, for example, a great manifestation of popular discontent boiled up—and fizzled out—in the Chartist Movement in the 1840's; and all through Europe, 1848 was a year of revolution. True, the main aims of these upheavals were political—to end dynastic absolutism and introduce the franchise. But in each of them a more radical left wing demanded not simply political change but a complete remolding of economic conditions and property relations which were felt to be intolerable. Of all the demands and programs put forward at that time, none was more cogent, hard-hitting, all-embracing, radical, yet visionary than Marx's *Communist Manifesto* published just as the revolutionary wave in Europe began to flow strongly toward the crest of 1848.

It is one more of the many paradoxes of history that Communism, which was to draw its strength from the miseries and aspirations of the masses, was the product not of any working-class leader but of a middle-class German intellectual of Jewish stock. The miseries were apparent to any one who cared to look, the aspirations were normal human aspirations—to live and eat and perhaps prosper. What turned the churning eddies of hate and hope into one of the greatest revolutionary forces of all time was the imagination and intellectual formulation provided by a single man. Marx found a world in the striving confusion of early industrialism and imposed upon it the order of his Communist idea.

And here we see, in all its force, what the idea, working in history, can bring about. A pattern of thought is derived by human imagination from certain given conditions—in Marx's case, the early decades of industrial growth. But once the pattern is established, it cuts loose from any necessary connections with reality. It exists in its own right. It can long survive the conditions which prompted it. It becomes a creator or a destroyer in all manner of new conditions, many of which it has helped to bring about. And so we have another paradox. One of the basic ideas of Communism is that environment and economic substructure create ideas. Yet no system of thought has ever so conclusively shown that, on the contrary, ideas modify and transform the economic and social substructure.

This potency of ideas to transform reality is one dimension of human freedom. But like all mankind's greatest gifts, it carries an opposite risk—that ideas become prisons in which people isolate themselves from any reality that does not fit into their own preconceived pattern. Presented with the choice between their theories and the facts, the blinded ideologues choose the theory and let the facts go hang.

Communism is already a hundred years old. Yet its fundamental presuppositions about industrial society have not changed in spite of all the radical changes

that have occurred in industrial society. The gap between the Communist view of the world and the world
as it actually is thus widens every day. It is a rift in
which humanity itself may founder.

II

What are these presuppositions? Perhaps before I
outline them, I should allow for one possibility. Are
we conceivably living in the final decades of pure
Communist orthodoxy? The appearance of Titoism on
the world stage and all the current discussions of "different roads to socialism" may presage the beginnings
of a whole spectrum of Communist faiths, allied yet
different, as are the sects of Christianity. We can still
talk of Communist orthodoxy today. But in twenty
years' time, shall we be able to say so emphatically
what Communism is? This I hold to be one of the
most encouraging signs that we shall not all be drawn
over the edge of the ideological abyss.

But today we can still discern an orthodoxy worked
out by Marx and by his friend Engels during the
period of nascent industrialism. Communism is thus
permeated through and through with reflections from
early industrial Britain. There are other influences—
German philosophy, French sociology, eighteenth-cen-
tury rationalism. But the solid underpinning of factual
study and social experience is provided in large measure
by the reactions of Engels and Marx to industrial
England in the Victorian period. It is much easier to

grasp some of the key factors in Communism if one realizes the extent to which they reflect this environment of a hundred years ago.

I cannot hope in a brief essay to give any idea of the full scale of Communist theory. I can only hope to pick out one or two points which are relevant to its subsequent development and to its growth as a world force.

The starting point is a theory of the dynamics of history. Marx believed, as we have seen, that the decisive element in human destiny is the material condition under which people work for their living. All else— politics, philosophy, religion—consists of so many reflections or projections of underlying material relationships—of the way property is divided, of techniques of production, and methods of exchange. There is a religion, an art, a system of government for communal, tribal agriculture, another for slave-owning society, another for feudalism and again another for capitalism, as each order of production gives way, by the dialectic of history, to its successor.

I do not think we need to elaborate this question of the dialectic which Marx took over from Hegel. It is roughly the idea that each condition tends to produce its opposite and out of this tension, a new synthesis arises. In the unfolding of history one set of economic relationships, say, feudalism with its dominant landowners, gives rise to the opposite and conflicting interest of merchants and bankers and nascent industrialists.

The next stage of society is already foreshadowed in the struggles over power and privilege and economic control—in other words the class struggle—of the previous epoch. The new class wins and the stage is set for the next phase of development.

In Marx's own day, Communism, he thought, was already stirring in the womb of early capitalism and however terrible and prolonged the convulsions attending its birth, it would triumph because it represented the irresistible force of determined history. But at this point, the dialectic would have done its work and history could cease. All previous class struggles had, in Marx's definition, been based upon the exclusive control of property by privileged groups. But if all ownership became public, if separate economic classes could no longer manipulate the levers of economic power in their own interest, all tension would die away; and with tension, change; and with change, history itself.

There is, one must admit, a certain magnificence in this picture of human destiny unfolding ineluctably through stage after stage of economic and social development to its appointed end in the classless millennium. The fact that most of the human race had not in fact traversed the great Marxian cycle from tribalism to slavery to feudalism to capitalism was not allowed to disturb the general harmony of this vast historical vision. At one time, Marx did consider "the Asian mode of production" as a possible variant to the general rule, but later on the concept was swept under the rug.

This point has more significance than Marxists care to admit. For what is this "Asian mode of production" but that method of large-scale, centralized, planned production which, as we have seen, underlay many of the great despotisms of the past? It is thus arguable that the kind of collective structure established in such societies as Russia or China has nothing whatsoever to do with the Marxian dialectic but is simply the adaptation to modern industry of an economic structure normal to Eastern society.

But there was a more immediate flaw in Marx's analysis. His picture of socialism struggling to be born as capitalism destroyed itself by its own contradictions was profoundly influenced by the first phase of capital accumulation in the West. He drew from the first five or six decades of industrialism conclusions which he generalized to cover the whole development of industry under more or less private ownership. In fact, as the century advanced the conditions in Western industrial society were to change, leaving the theory high and dry above the receding facts. Needless to say, Marx kept the theory, not the facts.

The most vulnerable point in the theory, as it turned out, was the "progressive immiseration of the workers" —in other words, the claim that as industry developed, the workers would grow steadily poorer and more wretched. How did Marx come upon this idea? Actually it is not an impossible conclusion to draw from the first brutal phase of capital growth—it was certainly true later on, for instance, of the period of the first Five Year Plan in Russia. During this phase, the workers coming in from the country, unused to industrial conditions, ignorant, brutalized, dwelling miserably in slums hastily run up for the purpose, work at a bare minimum necessary for survival while the entire increment is removed to create more capital, more machines, more enterprise. In a private society, private enterpreneurs make this transfer and reward themselves and their backers handsomely in the process. In a collective society, the Commissars do the transferring and look after themselves quite adequately, too. And in both cases, it does seem as though the misery of the masses is increasing as the capital for tomorrow's wealth is squeezed out of their labor.

Marx further remarked that competition between industrialists was beginning to produce mergers, larger units, even monopolies. From this he concluded that while the misery of the masses deepened, the number of men directly profiting at the top would steadily decrease. More and more miserable workers would face fewer and fewer rapacious monopolists. The day would come when the masses, fully class-conscious at last, would realize their strength, drive out the few owners, and transfer to the people the means of production whose control by private interests had led to the enrichment of the few at the expense of the many. In

Marx's limpid phrase, "the expropriators would be expropriated," and the golden age would begin.

All this was, of course, to come about automatically. The inescapable dialectic of history—an unbending goddess of iron countenance—cannot be revoked. Yet Marx was not above giving history a bit of a nudge. However inevitably Communism would emerge from capitalism, he realized that some of the "expropriators" would probably object to their own elimination and it might therefore be necessary to give history a little help. The change could, in short, be violent and during the interim period, which fits rather uneasily into the precise pattern of the dialectic, the workers might need to consolidate their power by maintaining a dictatorship of the proletariat. This, however, would be a temporary phenomenon and with the full establishment of Communism—of the public ownership of all the means of production—not simply the dictatorship of the proletariat but the state itself would "wither away."

One does not need to be a constitutional specialist to be amazed at the blithe way in which Marx waves away the risk of continued despotism. In time and space, absolute government is the customary method of exercising political power. No other tradition is known in Asia. Europe's own history of freedom is checkered with relapses into absolutism and in our own day produced the most extreme variants of dictatorship known to man. But we have to understand Marx's special angle of constitutional vision. He was very Victorian in his approach to government. Like Cobden and Bright, he did not think it had much function beyond that of preserving law and order and, as such, he saw it simply as a "managing committee of the bourgeoisie," as an instrument of class interest and class protection.

One can see why. The task of preserving law and order in Victorian times very often did mean sitting hard on the heads of those who wanted to change the order and were not too keen on the law—which, whatever else it did, certainly ensured the sanctity of property. If the state is seen chiefly in this policemen's role, protecting private property and interests, it is not illogical to assume that it will wither away when there is no more private property to protect. The government has in fact a thousand other functions, and so the logic seems to us to have the inner coherence and external fantasy of the lunatic. But many of the state's functions have been added since Marx's day. His political theory—like many of his economic theories —reflects conditions which are now a century out of date.

III

It did not take many decades to show that Marx's fundamental law of increasing misery was somehow failing to work out. For one thing, the industrial system was beginning to produce goods so much more effectively and cheaply that the new prosperity did in fact "trickle down." Between the 1860's and the early 1900's, prices fell, real wages rose, there was a noticeable increase in working-class prosperity.

Nor were the changes solely due to industrial expansion. Marx dismissed the influence of political institutions. They were derivative, he thought, and could not alter the substance of society. He therefore completely misunderstood the significance for Western industrial society of adult suffrage. One thing certain in any industrial system is that there will tend to be a majority of workers. If you extend the vote to all adults, this large group is bound to have some say in what is to happen. They are unlikely to be attracted by the proposal of steady general impoverishment and have no inhibitions about using the government they are beginning to influence in order to avoid such a gloomy outcome. It is no coincidence that in Britain with every extension of the franchise to the general body of voters, the state began to intervene more directly in the community's activities. Disraeli came to office in 1874 with the slogan: "Sanitas, sanitas, omnia sanitatum"—which might be interpreted not as "bread and circuses" but as "drains and housing"—and with him begins the welfare state.

Once the government is pledged to the provision of more and more services for the mass of the community, its sources of revenue have to increase. Progressive taxation makes its appearance and becomes steadily heavier. The rich become poorer and the poor become richer—as direct a contradiction of Marx's axiom as human reason can conceive. In short, under the impact of democracy and the vote, politics did what they had no right to do—altered the economic underpinning of the community.

This was not the only disobliging failure of society to confirm to Marx's pattern. Another deviation could be found in the growing power of independent trade unions. Far from being content with the old Iron Law of Wages—which held that competition between workers always thrusts wages down to the minimum necessary to keep a working class in being—the trade unions began to agitate steadily for increased wages, for better working conditions, and for shorter hours —aims in which they were supported by the more enlightened sectors of public opinion. In fact, Christian men of the stamp of Lord Shaftesbury led the campaign for factory reform even before the trade unions had the necessary influence to work for it themselves.

Successful trade union activity had more than economic consequences. To the disgust of the Marxists, some of the most active and "class conscious" of the new working-class leaders drew from their experience the political conclusion that industrial society needed not so much overthrow as reform. They wanted to advance toward a society in which wealth would be shared, in which brotherhood would be the rule of life, and in which great social differences would be abolished. But they believed that their vision of a socialist society could be achieved by peaceful argument and by the ballot box.

No belief has roused Marxists to greater fury. As in some forms of religious controversy, you can forgive a man who does not share your faith but there is no pardon for someone who claims to have a better variant. Communists have a quite special virulence for Socialists who say in effect: "We can do everything you can do better." The dispute still rages today. "Revisionism" is the crime of Socialists who, like Tito, believe that there may be more than one road—and some of them peaceful—to socialist society. In unalloyed Marxist theory —as interpreted today by Moscow and Peking—the notion of different paths is still anathema.

To return to the Law of Increasing Poverty—by the beginning of the twentieth century it took a good deal of swallowing. Economically, no facts were available to demonstrate it. Politically, it had been nullified by the emergence in the working class of cautious, reformist, antirevolutionary leaders who felt they had a real stake in industrial society. Clearly the theory had either to be explained or explained away.

IV

It was at this point that Lenin made his most significant contribution to the development of the Marxist canon. From scattered hints and comments of the master he elaborated a new theory to cover the obstinate refusal of Europe's workers to grow poorer and at the same time extended the whole range of Communist tactics and activity. Marx had always seen his theory as encompassing all mankind, but his chief focus had been Europe at the time of its industrialization. Lenin outlined more concretely the manner in which a worldwide revolution could be brought about.

The *Communist Manifesto* cannot be understood apart from the conditions of early industrialism; nor can Lenin's *Imperialism: The Highest Stage of Capitalism* be grasped out of context. When it was published in 1916 the major industrial Powers were at war or on the brink of it. Millions in Europe were fighting and dying to preserve, as they believed, their national independence and identity. Since between them they held in colonial control virtually the whole of Asia and Africa, the repercussions of the struggle stretched to the ends of the earth. From this vast maelstrom of war, nationalism, and colonialism, Lenin drew out a single pattern of interpretation which, because it seemed to explain everything, gained power over men's minds—just as Marx's hypnotic simplicities had done forty or fifty years before.

Briefly put, the Leninist theory of imperialism amounts to this: Since capitalism does not share its wealth with the workers, the home market soon reaches saturation and industrialists are bound to seek for fresh markets and new areas of profitable investment elsewhere. These in turn—in India, in Indonesia, in Africa—are ruthlessly exploited under colonial control. However, the wealth squeezed from them has percolated in some degree to the workers at home. Thus the law of increasing misery in Europe was mitigated by its application to colonial lands. British workers as well as capitalists waxed fat on profits sweated from the Indian coolie.

Yet the number of colonial markets available is limited. The industrialists must struggle to control them and their rivalry must lead inevitably to imperialist war. If, however, the colonial peoples could become conscious of their national rights and cast out the colonial expropriators and exploiters, their revolt would begin to break capitalism where its organization was most frail and could lead from nationalist to Communist revolution. Incidentally, capitalism in this theory did not need to exercise actual political control in order to be "imperialist." Simple foreign investment created exploitation. Thus in 1914 Russia was held to be a semicolonial dependency of Western finance capital because of the scale of foreign investment under Czarism.

You can see that this theory explained far more than Europe's failure to grow poorer. It explained why wars were inevitably caused by capitalism. It explained why capitalists had to have colonies. It explained why the Communist revolution could begin in such industrially backward countries as Russia—or China—whereas Marx seems to have expected the first breakthrough to occur in a fully developed industrial society. But after the Leninist definition of imperialism, it could be claimed that Russia was simply the "weakest link" in the capitalist chain. Later, the same explanation could serve for China.

The fact is, of course, that in both Russia and China, the Communist seizure of power had little or nothing to do with capitalism. In both countries, leaders of tactical genius had the sense to abandon the Marxist strategy of revolt based upon a developed industrial working class—which did not exist—and to exploit the two real sources of revolutionary ferment which did —war-weariness and the peasants' longing for land. It is a revealing sidelight on Marxist perspicuity that Stalin so misunderstood the lessons of Lenin's success in 1917 that he almost destroyed Chinese Communism by advising it to strike first in the cities through the almost minute urban working class. Only when Mao Tse-Tung took Communism to the peasants was it possible for Chinese Communism to find its road to victory.

Even in 1916, there were a lot of flaws in the Leninist argument. Most colonies had been acquired long before industrialism began and even where capitalism and colonialism appeared together, as in Africa, the Great Powers' rivalry there after 1880 had more to do with prestige and strategy than with the search for markets. Although colonial and maritime rivalry added something to the estrangement of Britain and Germany between 1880 and 1914, World War I was primarily fought, like all Europe's pre-industrial wars, to preserve the Balance of Power—in other words, to safeguard national survival.

The incongruities of Lenin's theory were not confined to Europe. America, the area where capitalism at that time was becoming most "monopolist," passed through and left behind a short fever of external intervention—in the Caribbean and the Pacific—invested marginally overseas and derived its growing prosperity from within its own wide boundaries. In fact, virtually every industrial country gained more of its wealth by conducting trade with developed industrial partners than by any colonial activity. Western Europe was a more valuable market for Britain than all Asia and Africa combined.

Yet in the twenties and thirties, this Leninist version of the Communist faith exercised a profound influence upon thought and policy. For one thing, the human mind, especially in a scientific era, has a bias against two explanations where one will do. Marxism-Leninism answers a profound instinct: to find a single pattern of explanation for everything—and there were enough facts available in the interwar years to fit the theory without too much violence.

Colonial control was a fact and, as we have already remarked, the economic policies of the European powers disrupted some Asian economies and failed to create conditions of dynamic expansion in others. There was enough discontent and frustration about for the charge of exploitation to be eagerly accepted. The discontent increased when in 1929 the capitalist world underwent a supreme crisis of overproduction and in the consequent depression, widespread dislocation and unemployment almost suggested that the law of increasing misery was at work after all.

Above all, the Marxists scored a master stroke in identifying "late-capitalism" with Fascism and using this identification to "prove" that capitalists must be war-mongers and imperialists. In fact, Fascism is the extreme point not of capitalism but of nationalism. Mussolini built the first working model in Italy, one of the least industrialized nations in Europe. The mature capitalist economies, Britain and America, which, if there is any such thing as late-capitalists, were undoubtedly the latest of all, remained immune to the supposed fatalities of their stage of economic development. Fascism sprang up in Italy and Germany, two nations distinguished not by the advanced stage of their capitalism but by the early stage of their nationalism. Both had waited longest to achieve that coincidence of frontiers and language which is one of the strongest roots of modern nationalism. Belated nationalism, not late capitalism, was their trouble. Their sense of nationhood was still febrile and insecure. Nationalist grievances, great-power illusions, the memory of military humiliation—these fevers, and not any hidden economic motives, drove the dictators on to war.

V

In spite of these obvious incongruities, Marxist-Leninist theory still kept a vestigial anchorage in the facts between the wars. It is since 1945 that the last link with reality has been broken and Communism has become a source of almost pure unreason in the world. Remember that its world picture has not changed. Advanced capitalist countries are still portrayed as ravening imperialists driven by the fear of overproduction at home to fight each other for control of markets abroad. They are still seeking to check the rise of local nationalism and to enslave the rest of the world either by direct domination or by the sinister economic control exercised through their overseas investments. They are still plotting war against the peace-loving guardians of the new Socialist order in Russia and China—even though it is not yet two decades since they fought at Russia's side.

These are the staple themes of Communist propaganda. Worse, this is the world of fantasy Communist leaders apparently inhabit and from which they draw their conclusions about policy. It is a sobering thought that for all their force and shrewdness men like Khrushchev and Chou En-lai may well be alienated from reality to a degree which would probably consign them, in private society, to a mental asylum.

Consider the actual, factual condition of the world today. The Western industrial powers have undergone no violent convulsions of overproduction. Mild recessions there have been, and these have had some repercussions abroad; but in general the upward surge of production in the mature industrial societies has actually exceeded earlier phases of industrial growth. We cannot say that the inherent tendency of capitalist economies to proceed by slump and boom—by alternations of under- and overproduction—has been entirely overcome. Perhaps this last Marxian contradiction is still with us. But at least, Western governments are now committed politically to policies which prevent the cycle from becoming catastrophic. The popular vote and Keynesian economics have made "full employment" the formal policy of Western democracy.

As a consequence of this economic expansion at home, there are no vast sums of capital competing for overseas markets and investment. On the contrary, America's foreign ventures are barely one-fifth of Britain's in the heyday of foreign lending and Britain itself is tempted to concentrate its investment at home. Shortage of capital is the world's trouble today, not the struggles of rival capitalists to go out and invest. Even where there are heavy Western investments—of which, of course, the chief is in oil—no Western Power is carving out oil territories under its own colonial control. On the contrary, Western policy in the Middle East can best be understood as a fumbling rearguard action to obtain even minimum safeguards for existing investment.

Nowhere is the gap between the Communists' world picture and the actual reality of things greater than in their political analysis of imperialism. Today, outside Africa, there are only pockets left of Western colonial control—tiny enclaves like Hongkong or Goa or Macao. In Africa itself Ghana's achievement of freedom is only the first act in an unfolding drama of African independence. Save in the Union of South Africa, even the communities of mixed racial stock are moving, however hesitantly, towards the eventual enfranchisement of the African majority. In the Arab world, only Algeria—another plural society—is still directly controlled from Europe. Yet in 1945 virtually the whole of Asia, Africa, and the Middle East was under Western colonial administration.

An earthquake, a cataclysm on a global scale, has occurred in the disappearance of so vast a dominion. The peacefulness of most of this gigantic transfer of power may have blinded people to its revolutionary character. Even so, there is a staggering unreality in the Communists' cries of imperialism and colonialism. The Law of Increasing Imperialism—if one may so paraphrase their insistent propaganda—is as ludicrous as the old Law of Increasing Misery.

Yet it confronts the world with a disturbing dilemma. It is perfectly possible to argue that the Communists' use of imperialism as a stick to beat the West is quite cynical. They believe that nationalist regimes emerging from a long period of colonial control are likely to be weak, divided and uncertain. The experience of Indonesia or Burma has done nothing to modify this judgment. In the new fluid situation, the Communists can hope to gain ground and sooner rather than later replace the nationalist regime that immediately succeeded the old imperial regime. They have everything to gain by pressing for independence and by continuing to paint a picture of a Western Imperialism that is ever ready to pounce again and reimpose the old control. Anti-imperialist propaganda is thus a simple instrument of ultimate Communist domination and non-Communist nationalist leaders—a Nasser or a Nehru or a Nkrumah —simply act as unwitting precursors to full Communist "liberation."

But it is also possible that the Communists' propaganda is not entirely cynical. They may be victims of it themselves. They may not simply find it more convenient to see the retreating West as the advance guard of imperialism. They may actually believe in a world-wide imperialist plot. Driven not by opportunism but by fear, they may move within a lurid global vision of Western menace and aggression, in a state of perpetual military preparedness, heavily armed, massively mobi-lized, scaring the death out of most other Powers and keeping the world for ever on the dreadful brink that overlooks Armageddon.

This state is not imcompatible with what we know of mental alienation. Fear and aggression are twin sides of the same coin of hallucination. The Com-munists may fear the West, but they have not aban-doned the original Marxist goal of a total Communist world order. How, then, can one distinguish the offen-sive from the defensive aspects of their policy, how determine whether conciliation designed to check Communist fears will not be interpreted as softness inviting a Communist assault? Western diplomacy may have been something less than skillful in handling the Communist phenomenon, but let no one suppose that there is any easy, straightforward method of dealing with the rulers of nine hundred million people who behave as though they believed that men stand on their heads or that the sun goes round the earth—or the equivalent, that the Western Powers are plotting imperialist war and world dominion.

Communism, in short, is the tragedy of ideas working free from the reasonable restraint of fact. In Marx's own day, its entire analysis and strategy were based upon the first phase of capitalist accumulation—a grim period in any society. In the Leninist aftermath, its doctrines were fashioned in the last phase of Western colonialism. Today, both phases are a matter of history. Western capitalism has evolved far beyond its painful beginnings. Western imperialism is being liquidated more rapidly—and on the whole more peacefully— than any comparable dominion in the human record. But Communism keeps pounding along, repeating the same slogans and proclaiming the same myths as though the whole march of events had been arrested at the moment at which Marx and then Lenin turned a baleful eye on Western society. The gap between ideology and fact thus grows wider every hour, and like all demonstrations of unreality, it grows more dangerous. Unanchored in anything save power, fear, ambition, and fantasy, who can say to what risks and follies it may not seduce the leaders of the Communist world?

VI

How, then, has an order of ideas, a doctrine, an ideology patently at variance with the facts contrived to become one of the greatest revolutionary forces ever known to man? The answer, I believe, has very little to do with Communist orthodoxy but everything to do with the concrete experience of the Soviet state. In 1914, Russia was about to go through the "sound barrier" of modern capitalism. The fearsome privations and turmoil of early industrialism still lay heavily on the country, and the degree of capital accumulation was not yet sufficient to transform industrialization from an iron penance for all save the few to a means of greater prosperity for everyone.

The First World War ruined what had been begun. By 1917, the whole fragile structure of Czarist Russia, caught between a dying and an unborn order of society, collapsed. The universal confusion gave Lenin and his determined Bolshevik minority the opportunity to seize power. Then they found themselves in charge of a vast country but with no doctrines that seemed to apply. Marx had expected revolution to occur only when a full-scale industrial apparatus, created by the bourgeoisie, was already in being. None existed in Russia in 1918. The Bolsheviks tried pure Communism for a time, putting workers in charge of factories. It did not work. To keep some feeble pulse stirring in the country Lenin had to restore a measure of free enterprise under his New Economic Policy, and I think one can safely say that if Russia policy had advanced no further than the confusions of its first decade, we should have heard little of Communism as a worldwide force.

Stalin's contribution was the forced-draft industrialization of Russia. He combined two traditions—the industrial experience and techniques worked out under private enterprise in the West and the traditional "Asian method of production" based upon centralized control, state planning, and a vast bureaucracy. Under such stringent political control, there seemed no limit to the amount of saving that could be shorn from the people. The thirties were a time of bloody oppression and misery for millions of Russians. But the basis of a vast industrial apparatus was laid—and laid in time to resist the Nazi invasion.

Nor was it simply a physical achievement. Communism provided the element of zeal, discipline, and almost Puritanical fervor which had distinguished the earlier Calvinist attitude toward the creation of wealth. In the great drive to modernize the country, no resources—either human or material—were neglected. Education was made universal, the curriculum redesigned for modern scientific society; able children were forced forward up the ladder of learning, the university became the entry to the new elite.

For thousands of workers, for the ignorant peasants coming in from the countryside, for the bewildered tribesmen of Uzbekistan or Khirgizia, the new industrial world was as alien and hideous as the worst slum in Glasgow or Pittsburgh. According to one estimate, as many workers were killed in the building of Magnitogorsk as in the Battle of the Marne. But for their children there was the chance for a new existence, and by clearing away the old aristocratic Czarist superstructure, the Communist leaders had thrown open these chances to more people than had any previous way of life.

The appeal of Communism is not so much its dialectic or its metaphysics—save to a minute group of intellectuals in search of a new faith—but its ability to carry backward countries speedily through the tremendous crisis of modernization. It offers a successful pattern of industrial saving and it provides the drive and discipline without which saving, particularly in poor countries, cannot be achieved. It also promises that the fruits of the transformation will ultimately be enjoyed "by each according to his need."

This last promise cannot yet be judged. Those who control the means of production—whether they are capitalists or bureaucrats—tend to reward themselves rather more handsomely than the mass of the people. Certainly, the gap between the Commissar and the day laborer in Russia is greater than between the average American manager and trade unionist. But compared with the gulf between rich and poor customary in pre-industrial society, the results of Communism already show it to be an instrument of radical justice as well as of technical innovation. We should not forget that Marx, for all his scientific jargon, was a prophet in the great Hebrew tradition, putting down the mighty from their seats and exalting them of low degree. In the misery and confusion of our present worldwide economic revolution, there are millions who will listen to his prophetic promises of justice who never heard of the dialectic and would not recognize a synthesis if they saw one.

It is not, therefore, difficult to grasp the appeal of Communism to backward areas of the world, to lands still living in misery and economic stagnation, plagued by ambitions toward a better lot, restrained by the traditions of pre-industrial society and the authority of older modes of leadership. In China, as we have seen, the wreck of the old Manchu system was followed by forty years of almost continuous war, during which the industrial transformation of society could hardly be carried through under middle-class leadership on the Western model, weakened as it was by inflation and by its association with "colonial" foreign capital. Communism was therefore able to repeat the Bolshevik tactic. It based itself on peasant discontent in a country sickened with war and destruction and, once in power, began to thrust through, with comparable rigor, the total modernization of the economy.

Must we, then, assume that the driving vigors and

simplicities of Communism offer the future pattern of modernization and that, at least outside the older industrial West, we face in Communism "the wave of the future"? There are, I believe, solid grounds for believing that the future is not so rigidly determined. Russia and China are great powers, the greatest powers in numbers and soon perhaps in resources that the world has seen. Communism in their powerful system does not entail being subjugated to anyone else, does not, in short, entail imperialism. But the fate of Eastern Europe suggests that Communism for smaller powers carries no such guarantee of independence and elbow room.

I do not myself believe that imperialism at this late day is going to become more attractive simply by calling itself "international proletarian solidarity." Hungary stands as the tragic proof that national independence and international Communism are not yet compatible. I suggest that this lesson is not lost on the nationalist leaders around the world who are supposed to be preparing Communism's advance.

Again, I do not believe that Communism as a system has yet shown us that it can do more than drive societies at breakneck speed through the "sound barrier" of modernization. But out on the other side, a thousand problems remain—above all, the problem of an economy flexible enough and sensitive enough to provide ordinary people with the things they really want. For this, the market economy is a much better instrument than

(147)

bureaucratic planning. Yet one may question whether the Communists will dare risk the step of making the consumer supreme, for this change might also enhance his position as a voter. How much choice can you admit economically without awkward questions of political choice arising too?

And here we touch on what, surely, remains the greatest failure and potential weakness of Communism. It is politically inflexible. It enshrines the principle of despotic authority in a world now shot through with the dreams, hopes, and experiences of free government. You cannot cancel this pressure and this ferment, any more than you can turn imperialism into something else by inventing new names for it. And this failure to confront the realities of politics has been, I believe, the fundamental flaw in Marx's thought from the very first hour.

He dismissed as irrelevant trappings the political traditions of Western life—the rule of law, constitutional practice, the vote, supremacy of parliament, the hard-won rights and liberties of the individual. But these were the means whereby Western industrial society eased itself through the crises of early industrialism, sloughed off its colonial past and began, by trial and error and innovation and experiment, to turn industrialism into an instrument of well-being for more and more of its citizens while leaving them to enjoy the supreme good of individual rights and ordered liberty.

Communism misunderstands totally the central problem of power. By relying on such puerile fantasies as the "withering away of the state," it has allowed a concentration of political and economic power to come about in the Communist state which goes even beyond the oriental tyrannies that are its model. Power still corrupts; absolute power still corrupts absolutely, and Khrushchev's recital of Stalin's iniquities at the 20th Party Congress was only one more dreary record of the despot's traditional cruelties and crimes.

Nor is it only the domestic community which bears the terrible risks and penalties of unfettered power. The Government which respects no limits on its internal authority tends to be equally lawless in its external relations. The Soviet and Chinese governments, for all their internationalist protestations, stand firm on the principle of unlimited sovereignty and state power. And they do so in the atomic age when the unbridled right of all states to do exactly what they wish can lead inexorably to the holocaust that destroys them all.

Chapter Five

Internationalism

THE great paradox of this century is that we have reached an extreme pitch of national feeling all around the world just at the moment when, from every rational point of view, we have to find ways of progressing beyond nationalism. This point needs great emphasis because, in this field, our reason and our emotion probably do not work in the same direction.

Rationally, we can add up all the reasons why we should be looking towards the creation of a genuine international society, but every single one of us feels the tug of separateness, of nationalism, of ultimate loyalties devoted exclusively to our own community and not concerned with that wider, larger, and admittedly vaguer community of mankind. The natural instinct is to feel united and identified with one's own group, and to forget any wider kinship. We have therefore to rally all that we have of reason and clarity and common sense and look at our world not through a haze of national emotions but see it as it is, in cold, hard, reality.

The first fact about our world is that owing to the activities of the scientist, the industrialist and the technician, it is, in a very real sense, physically one world. We can travel round it in many ways more quickly than our forefathers could travel, say, in Europe or the United States a hundred years ago. We have seen the conquest of space; the aeroplane is a commonplace, and more and more people are using this means of transport. Yet it is in itself undergoing radical change and the speeds of today are nothing to the supersonic speeds of tomorrow. With each thrust of the new jet engines, our physical proximity is increasing.

And as aircraft increase in size, the cost of travel diminishes. Millions use the air today. Millions more will use it tomorrow. Mobility and accessibility are replacing the old rooted, isolated existence of mankind from one end of the globe to the other.

We are also drawn together by the interconnectedness of our world economy. I need hardly point out that in Ghana the great works of development which we all hope to see accomplished—and which include such promising institutions as the new University—depend directly upon the movements of the world market for cocoa, and on the promise but also on the vagaries and uncertainties of the export trade.

This is true of Ghana; it is also becoming true of every nation in the world. The first aim of countries which 'are still cut off from the main commercial currents by the continuance of a local subsistence economy is to industrialize, to increase their export trade, and, in short, to be drawn into the web of an international economy in which we are all more or less enmeshed.

To this new proximity we must now add a new and appalling dimension. Even if it is a commonplace, we must try by all means to keep our sense of shock and dismay, for here at least is one idea to which mankind must never become reconciled. This new fact is, of course, that we can destroy ourselves utterly and completely, that we can, by launching a hydrogen war, in all probability put an end to the human species.

This is a totally new risk. Wars in the past have been terrible and wasteful, they have led to the wiping-out of whole civilizations, to the ruin and annihilation of peoples, to destruction beyond name. Yet never, never before could it even be thought that from a war no remnant of humanity would survive. Today, the ending of the human experiment is one of the possibilities of life before us and petty indeed should all our local differences seem compared with the basic challenge of

(153)

human survival. To the community of conquered space and economic interdependence we have thus added a community of potential destruction. Color, race, class, ideology—these differences vanish as we all stand in our stark, basic equality as mortal men facing the risk of extinction.

These are the realities of our world which no amount of thinking or hoping or believing can turn aside. They are with us; they are the daily bread of our international affairs. Surely it is no more than reasonable to say that priority over every other problem in the world must now be given to achieving the minimum institutions which will enable us not to encompass our own destruction.

But having agreed so far, we have also to admit that the record of humanity thus far is hardly encouraging. Throughout man's checkered history, one common feature has been revealed from his tribal origins down to the present day: that men fight each other, and that war is endemic; it is the oldest, as well as the most savage, institution of mankind. Therefore—and here is another paradox of our century—we have to do away with our oldest institution because of the newest of our discoveries.

Yet the old is rooted in our deepest instincts; above all, in the belief that each group has the right to have its own way. If you do not think that this instinct is deeply rooted, I would implore you to observe any child between the ages of six months and four years, and see the absolute determination with which it pursues its own desires. Those bashings on the nursery floor are the first early signs of the instinct we carry right on into the organization of our adult society—the instinct to have our own way with the things we most want. Organized at the state level with the passion of nationalism behind it—and possibly of ideology as well —we have not a rational institution but a battering-ram of disorderly desires.

In fact, it can be argued that nationalism is to communities what egoism is to human beings. It may destroy us but we cling to it as to our last defense. In our world society we cherish the idea that our own group, our own nation shall be able, in the last resort, to have its own way. Since every other group has the same determination, the ultimate clash is pretty well unavoidable. There is unhappily a certain basic, dreary simplicity about the fact of war, and we can pursue it back to its roots in human nature.

Nevertheless, one of the encouraging signs in the evolution of civilized societies over the last two or three thousand years, is that we have, within our domestic society, reached some conclusions about the best methods of preventing lawless violence—which, after all, is what war is. We prevent this violence inside the state by two or three crucial acts of policy. First of all, we give up the right to settle our own disputes by force. Whatever we may think of the rights and the wrongs of our disagreements, we settle them by nonviolent means

—by arbitration or through law.

Yet because human nature is frail, and the temptation to knock the other fellow on the head remains very strong, we also accept the necessity of a police force to ensure that neither we nor others revert to private violence in pursuit of our own ends. A force independent of individual influences and desires, linked to the system of judicial control, reinforces our sometimes wavering decision not to take the law into our own hands. It also protects us from anyone else who might succumb to the temptation. These are key institutions in the prevention of private violence within domestic society, and perhaps the greatest effort of imagination we have to make today, when we stand face to face with the risk of possible destruction, is to see that war, too, is private violence—private violence committed on the body of the human race.

The framework of justice is not, however, sufficient in itself to banish violence. We also know from domestic society that there are certain conditions which lend themselves very easily to commotion and disorder, or at the extreme degree, to civil strife in which the whole compact of domestic peace breaks down. Such conditions are more likely to prevail when legitimate ambitions are thwarted, when misery is widespread, when hopes are deferred, and whole communities feel that they have no chance of maintaining themselves or their children above the level of want and misery.

In the last hundred years, I would say that one of

the great insights of free society in the West has been to realize that there is little hope of a peaceful society if it is not a just and progressive society as well. We have seen that welfare is the prop of justice and that those societies in which civil peace can best be maintained are those in which there is reasonable hope, reasonable stability, and in which parents can look forward to giving their children at least as good a life as they have had themselves or possibly better. In short, a community of well-being within domestic society is one of the soundest underpinnings of social peace.

In one sense this is not perhaps a new insight. Western civilization has always been haunted by the vision of a just and compassionate human order. Western democrats and Western Communists both draw on the apocalyptic vision of the Bible in which "God shall wipe away all tears from their eyes; and there shall be no more death, neither sorrow nor crying, neither shall there be any more pain: for the former things are passed away." But in a static, subsistence economy, the physical means of banishing misery are strictly limited. Once a failure in the harvest or rising population alters the balance between what is needed and what is available, not even the utmost exertions of private charity can avert disaster. And in any case, charity was not always overactive.

With the coming of science and industry, however, the means for combating hopeless want came into existence. Poverty ceased to be a fatality. It could be countered once the economy had found its way through the "sound-barrier" of capital accumulation. Perhaps even today we are not fully aware of the revolutionary implications of this change. Inside Western democratic society, the principle of welfare has been enshrined and well-being more widespread than ever before. But we hesitate on the edge of their wider application—to the whole family of man.

If, now, we judge our need for international institutions on the basis of domestic experience, it would seem that three kinds are indispensable—the first to assure peaceful methods of settling disputes, the second to police the legal, peaceful solutions thus obtained and to avert fresh violence, the third to secure minimum conditions of economic well-being. The fact that we do, in some measure, admit the necessity of these institutions is shown by our hesitant steps toward their achievement. We have a United Nations, even though the great Powers' veto enshrines absolutely the principle that "beyond a certain point, I intend to have my way." We have made a first few marginal experiments in international policing, and at least we talk of disarmament, inspection, and control. We have set up a number of international organizations—the World Bank, for instance, or the Children's Fund—which recognize economic problems common to all humanity, irrespective of nationality or culture or race.

These are pointers. They show, perhaps, the direction

of our rational convictions. But they do not yet mark our settled policies and they are certainly far from providing the ordinary framework within which we seek to conduct our international affairs. Before we can decide how best to advance to more orderly conditions, we had better first take a dispassionate look at the disorders in which we are plunged today.

II

The first inescapable fact is the division of the world between two great military blocs bitterly distrustful, bitterly opposed to each other, and jockeying for support among the remaining third of mankind whose present anxiety on the whole seems to be to keep clear of the conflict. Of these two blocs, the Communist Powers are clearly the more expansive and aggressive force. Simply in physical terms of acres annexed and populations controlled, the extension of Russian power into Eastern Europe—or of Chinese into Central Asia— must be compared with the West's coincident and massive retreat from its old colonial holdings. No propaganda in the world can conceal the contrast when it comes to these concrete realities of power.

But the facts are easier to establish than the motives behind them. Up to a point, Russian action in Eastern Europe can be explained in terms of genuine strategic necessity. In the last four hundred years, Russia has been invaded with monotonous regularity by way of Eastern Europe and the two German invasions of the

Ukraine occurred within the living memory of men and women not yet much advanced beyond middle age. To ensure some new form of security in these border regions after the bloodshed and butchery of two great wars cannot be accounted irrational or illegitimate.

Here we come to the old problem—the degree to which the masters of the Kremlin are ridden not only by rational fear but by the irrational terrors of their own ideology. It would, after all, have been perfectly conceivable to impose what one might call the "Finnish solution" in Eastern Europe. The governments would have been allied to their Russian neighbor and would not have contained a majority hostile to Russia. But internal autonomy would have been respected and no attempt made to impose total Communist control through the instrument of a local minority Communist party. This solution has worked in Finland and could certainly have been attempted in cooperation with the mixed coalition governments established in Eastern Europe after the war. Certainly neither a Benes nor a Masaryk in Czechoslovakia would ever have pursued anti-Soviet policies.

Yet all these coalitions were tricked and forced out of power, the Communist minority was established in total control at the point of Soviet bayonets and proceeded to impose regimes which Khrushchev himself has admitted to have been systems of inhuman terror.

How is the outside world to account for such policies? If, on the basis of ideology, the Russian rulers actually believe that only Communists can be trusted and that every other form of regime is actually or potentially allied to "the Western imperialists," their actions have at least an internal logic even though it may not be related to external reality. But an alternative possibility must be considered—that they are determined to impose a Communist world order by fraud where possible, by force where necessary. This alternative has to be given all the more weight in view of the scale of armament the Russians have maintained since the war —armament which could be explained, on the fearful and defensive theory of Russian motivation, by America's possession of the atomic bomb, but which could alternatively be due to plans of conquest and expansion. The problem is made no simpler by the likelihood that both motives are about equally and strongly at work.

This is the bewildering situation the Western Powers have faced since World War II, and it is not one that fits easily into their contemporary ways of thinking. The first point to remember is that the leading nations in the West are not fired by any vision of world order or any dream of world dominion. In Europe imperialism is dead or in full retreat. In America it never got under way. The powers concerned are in the main prosperous. They want to trade. They do not want to control. In fact, their deepest instinct, as stable, satisfied powers, is to stay home and not be bothered.

I do not think, even now, that Western peoples are

really aware of the vast revolution their old colonialism and their new industrialism have launched in the world. They do not expect the political upheavals that must follow when a whole imperial order vanishes in a decade and states and leaders struggle for the succession. They want to believe in a world that runs itself and leaves them in peace.

In fact, if you were to give most of these Western peoples two wishes, I would hazard the guess that the first wish would be for the disappearance of all Communists and the second for the disappearance of all friends and allies. Then, with all external botherations eliminated, they could settle down and profitably mind their own business. You may think there is an element of caricature in this. I am not so sure. What is certain is that nothing in the West corresponds to the driving, expansive Communist vision of a world system under sole Communist control.

But the Western Powers cannot carry wish-fulfillment to the pitch of disregarding the challenge of Communist expansion. Wherever weakness and political instability have followed the end of imperialism—as in Burma or Indonesia—the Communists are at work making the instability unsteadier still. Where rampant nationalism is moving in—as with Nasser's Arab nationalism—the Communists work at one remove, encouraging national fanaticism in the hope of replacing it in due course. All this creates such a perpetual tremor of unrest under the earth's political crust that one does not need a very sensitive seismograph to fear the risk of earthquakes ahead. And the earthquake may explode into the mushroom cloud of the hydrogen bomb.

Here we reach the decisive point. The world can carry a certain amount of political disorder without its erupting into general disaster. Latin America, an area of successor states to the old Iberian colonialism, has taken a century to look for alternative stable methods of organization, and the search still goes on, to the accompaniment of considerable local disturbance. But the local parties are not—yet—linked to external forces and their disputes are naturally quarantined.

This is not the only pattern. In the Balkans before 1914, local leaders and local parties were struggling to fill the vacuum left by the decay of the old Turkish Empire. In this contest, two European Great Powers—Russia and Austria-Hungary—took sides. Twice it was possible to quarantine the local outbreaks. But in 1914 the restraints broke down and a Balkan political murder set in motion the outside mobilizations which led to general war. It would be idle to deny that comparable risks face us today wherever local instability invites or at least permits Great Power intervention.

I am not at this point allotting blame. Let us take the most generous view of Soviet motivation and admit that special defensive measures were reasonable in Eastern Europe. But in the same measure, we must admit the inevitability of the Western response. Apart from the atomic bomb—when America offered to internationalize—there was precipitate disarmament in the West between 1945 and 1948. It took the Greek Civil war, the Communist rape of Czechoslovakia, the establishment of Communist governments in Eastern Europe, the blockade of Berlin, and the whole scale of Russia's military establishment even to begin the process of rearmament in the West. It took the North Korean attack upon South Korea to confirm it.

Never forget how much of this response was dictated by recent memories of Hitler. Year after year, before 1939, Britain and France preferred to rely on Hitler's "good intentions" until finally it was all but too late to stop him. That experience seared itself across Western minds and when, after the war, the Soviet concentration of dictatorial power began pressing in upon Europe, the conviction grew that the mistake over Hitler must not be repeated. The Western Powers determined on a collective system of defense to check any further possibility of Soviet advance. Thus the North Atlantic Treaty Organization springs quite as much from memories of 1939 as from any menace of today and as such is very far from being an irrational response to the situation.

Collective security is based on the idea that if a group of nations band themselves together to defend each one of them against aggression, then collective force will deter the possible law-breaker. In a sense, it is a substitute for an international police force. Had the concept of collective security been applied on both sides of the Atlantic during the rise of Hitler, we should probably have been spared the horrors of the Second World War.

However, this Western response to the Russian combination of ideology, arms, expansiveness, and total dictatorship has brought into being two great rival blocs of power. This is less dangerous for the world's freedom than the existence of only one great bloc with overwhelming power. Yet it is superlatively dangerous all the same and threatens to repeat, in situation after situation, the uncontrolled Balkan spiral into general hostilities.

The risk has even been increased by the West's unwise decision to try to extend the concept of collective security to areas in which its relevance is much less obvious. In the Atlantic alliance, collective defense is based upon strong and independent industrialized nations which have learned in two terrible struggles the error of postponing defense too long. If they add their defensive force together, they increase it substantially and, in doing so, they are drawing directly upon their own very recent historical experience.

This situation is, however, strictly confined to the Atlantic area. In Asia, in Africa, in the Middle East, the immediate historical experience of most people, leaders and masses alike, is with the struggle for national independence. It is hard for nations to switch their minds to the problem of Russian efforts to come in when all their efforts until yesterday—and in some areas their present efforts too—have been concentrated upon compelling the British or the French or the Dutch to get out. As late as 1945, most of Asia, Africa, and the Middle East was ruled from London or Paris. Twelve years is a very short time in which to reverse national objectives entirely, and it is more difficult still to alter the whole emotional coloring of men's minds and instincts.

In fact, it probably cannot be done. The reactions of excolonial nations are bound for a time to resemble those of America after 1775. It would not be surprising if for fifty years or so, the natural responses of these areas were to continue to be a passionate desire to be left alone, a pervasive fear of intervention from the old quarter, and a fully formulated public policy of neutrality or, as it is now called, "non-alignment."

Their economic position reinforces this political outlook. In Europe, fully industrialized nations add something to each other's defensive strength. This is not the case in most other areas. There is virtually no industrialization in the Middle East or South East Asia. India, a giant in population, does not yet produce six million tons of steel a year. Africa, outside the Union, is almost completely pre-industrial. What defensive strength is gained by adding together powerless local units? Certainly nothing that could stand up for one hour to an invasion by Russia with or without nuclear weapons, always supposing that direct invasion is intended—which most of the neutral world does not or prefers not to believe.

It is true that a guarantee from the Western Powers does add significantly to local strength and in their secret hearts many neutral leaders are no doubt grateful that they are not left alone in the world to face one, single, overwhelming bloc of Soviet power. But the American counterweight to Russia exists whether or not it is invoked, and the last thing most small nations want is to bring it into action locally. To have the Great Powers fight on their soil will leave them annihilated. There is an African proverb: "When the bull elephants fight, the grass is trampled down." Many smaller states feel that the best method of avoiding catastrophe is simply to keep out of the bull elephants' way.

Nor can one say that their instinct for neutralism is obviously and dangerously unsound. Policies need the support of peoples, and it is almost impossible to pursue policies which go against the whole grain of local emotion. It is, for instance, hard to argue that the Baghdad Pact increased stability in the Middle East. It brought Britain back into the area of its earlier imperial control within a year or so of its supposed final departure. The aim was to counter the risk of Russian intervention—which did not seem particularly acute to the local peoples—but by creating a formal anti-Soviet bloc, it almost invited a Russian riposte. When it came, in the shape of Nasser's deal with the Soviets, the tide of Arab popular opinion was far more easily rallied against the old British imperialist everyone knew than alarmed over a new Soviet imperialist who so far had made no obvious encroachments. To crown the alienation of local opinion from Western policy, Britain and America were the sponsors of Israel, and Israel is the only enemy all Arabs are prepared to recognize.

Thus the Pact helped to exacerbate local tensions, invited Great Power interest and pressure on rival local sides, brought about a truly Balkan condition of instability. There is no need to recall how often in recent years the Middle East has taken the world to the brink of war. All in all, the attempt to extend the principle of collective security outside the Atlantic area in which it is valid in the historical and popular sense to regions where, on the whole, it is not, has added little to either local stability or local security. It may even have done the opposite by offering Russia new chances of infiltration and by alienating local nationalist opinion. Yet the problem of countering Communist pressure remains. Is there any alternative?

III

From all the discussions that have been conducted ceaselessly on the Middle Eastern issue in the last four or five years, elements of a coherent strategy can, of course, be drawn. Whether they can be applied is another matter, but the bare bones of a settlement are at least beginning to be recognized. The aim is to expand the role of local United Nations police forces already in the area sufficiently to ensure that the political changes which are bound to continue to occur in the Arab lands do not involve local war—above all, a war with Israel. Given a strengthened international force, the outside Powers could be required to cut short all warlike assistance to local states and, in fact, to accept the neutralization of the area from outside intervention.

At the same time, internal stability might be increased and the fires of nationalism somewhat damped by a really ambitious development program for the whole region, which would give the hotheads and the hungry and the unemployed something else to do. In part the resources involved would be drawn from oil revenues, in part from outside assistance. No one forgets the appalling poverty of Egypt, caught between rising births and static agricultural land, or the significant link between the Suez crisis and the Western Powers' deliberately discourteous announcement they would not help Nasser to finance the Aswan Dam.

The advantages of such an approach are obvious enough. It gives the area some security while removing it from the tensions and risks of Great Power rivalry. It provides the capital and technical aid needed to push a wretchedly backward region through the difficult early crises of economic growth and industrialization. It creates some sort of framework within which the uncertain aftermath of an old imperialism can be lived through without inviting the intervention of a new.

As a formula, indeed, it applies to other regions beside

the Middle East. It is relevant to all unsettled areas where political uncertainty, economic backwardness, and local aspirations keep a tempting pot boiling for outside interest to stir. If areas such as South East Asia or Latin America or Africa south of the Sahara could be withdrawn—or preserved—from Great Power competition, their economic growth reinforced by consistent long-term economic programs on a regional basis and local security strengthened by international forces to police any border disputes threatening the peace— for instance, the unsettled Chinese-Burmese frontier in the Shan states—a more coherent pattern of security could be brought into being than any that exists today.

There are many who argue that Europe, too, for all its industrial strength and ancient nationhood, has become a potential battleground between the mighty powers of Russia and America, and that stability will be impossible so long as the continent is divided between two hostile military coalitions. These fears are increased by two facts: one, that the division passes down the middle of a single powerful country, Germany; the other, that Russia's oppressive control of Eastern Europe has already produced two massive popular revolts. It is not to be assumed that all opposition has now ceased in this large colonial area nor that a recrudescence of revolt could always be quarantined as was the Hungarian uprising. Once Western Germany is armed again, a new revolt in East Germany might well call forth West German assistance, and it is not to be supposed that either great Power would leave its local client to face defeat. In fact, one can argue that "Balkan" possibilities of spiraling aggression reach their most acute point in Europe, and it is here that the process of disengagement should begin.

The risk is, of course, that the withdrawal of American forces across the Atlantic would be a total withdrawal, whereas the Russians, pulling back only to the Pripet Marshes, would then dominate the whole continent.

Theoretically it is possible to counter this danger. At present, American forces are no more than a "trip wire" in Europe. All the NATO armies put together could not check a determined Russian advance to the Channel, were such a plan in Soviet minds. But the presence of the thin American screen guarantees America's entrance into the conflict with its whole hydrogen striking force. Thus the deterrent today is not the local NATO garrison but the risk of stumbling over the trip wire.

In these conditions, it is not impossible to devise an alternative trip wire in the shape of a United Nations police force, stationed at strategic points in Europe which, by preserving the fact of the American deterrent, would guarantee the continent against the possibility of Russian re-invasion. Europe's security would still rest—

as it does today—on a balance of terror, but the local chances of setting the terror to work would be greatly reduced.

The theory, I believe, is sound. It is, perhaps, the ultimate aim which the NATO powers should set themselves, especially in these days when the development of intercontinental missiles is beginning to compel every strategist to reconsider his premises in a drastic way. But as an immediate solution, it cannot excite much hope. Now that the opposition of even Eastern Europe to Communism has become so patent, can we suppose that Russia will be ready to withdraw the Soviet garrisons which keep satellite governments propped up in their shaking seats? And on the Western side, General de Gaulle's apparent readiness to disrupt NATO and to rely on his own nuclear deterrent makes it exceedingly difficult for Western strategic planners to work out any policy in concert. De Gaulle may even be seeking "disengagement." Yet it seems to be chiefly the Americans he wishes to disengage. In theory, nevertheless, there is much to be said for limited experiments in disengagement. A broad neutral zone free of atomic weapons and policed by an international force along the length of the present dividing line might prove a first step in progressive disengagement and would reduce the immediate risk of a border explosion. Nor, if it were firmly undertaken as a first step only, would it formalize Russia's grip on Eastern Europe. In fact, now that Western Europe has consolidated its recovery and its confidence, the present danger seems to be that Western Europe may lose its essential unity and sense of direction under the prodding of the kind of separatist nationalism De Gualle has unleashed. If Communist Russia is not to exploit these new western divisions and thus recover the taste for expansion, the first need in the West is a fair British entry into the European Common Market, the creation of a democratic supra-national order in Western Europe and the working out of a viable and permanent partnership with the United States. Otherwise Communism will once again believe that it can divide and rule.

Yet tension in the disputed areas is not the end of the problem. Even if it is conceivable to introduce measures of international control into the twilight zones between the great centers of power, what is to be done about them? Is a balance of terror the best we can hope for? The day is not far distant when a technician in one hidden armory can touch a button which will destroy a continent half the world away. Are we then to live with only that measure of security that can be said to lie in the certainty that both sides can inflict planetary death? The prospect is uninviting enough for us to explore with all energy and all hope the possible alternatives.

I do not myself believe that programs of partial disarmament are the answer save in one particular. Any agreement which enshrines precise, detailed, and enforceable systems of international supervision is worth having, virtually for that reason alone. International inspection of the Polar regions, for instance, or international supervision of an end to nuclear tests breaks down the immunity of Great Powers to the workaday restraints of reason and humanity, and, in the case of Russia and China, dents the principle of total secrecy which, even more than their Communism, is a perpetual menace to mankind.

Partial disarmament, however, confronts the Powers with the daunting problem of what one might call the "shopping lists" of comparative disarmament. How many of my submarines are equal to a couple of your flattops? In the present debate on disarmament, a virtually insoluble example has arisen. Russia's insistence upon banning nuclear weapons—a cry that echoes in every human heart—conceals this gimmick, that the abolition of atomic arms leaves supreme the man with the tank; and the Russians—and the Chinese—have thousands of tanks and millions of men. For starting a war, a tank is as handy as a bomb, but the peculiar horror of atomic weapons has—understandably—hypnotized men's minds. Irrationally, they are not so hypnotized by mass armies and massed armor. The Russians have thus earned a psychological dividend by directing the debate to the weapons most relied on in the West and away from the weapons and manpower solidly underpinning the East.

One can, certainly, criticize the Western strategy for relying on atomic firepower and letting military manpower be whittled away. It is entirely possible that the Western Powers today need more highly mobile, highly trained police units rather than yet more bombs. Little wars are more likely than big wars, and men with moderate weapons win the moderate wars.

Yet can one really lay final blame on the West for allowing their men to demobilize? What virtue is there in vast militarized nations, with millions of men under the restraint of military discipline and millions more trained for armed action, as "volunteers," for instance, in other peoples' disputes? If our universe could be viewed in a rational light, it would be apparent that there is more menace in a swollen Chinese or Soviet military establishment than in an American armory of atomic weapons—especially when we remember that the Russians have both.

No—the difficulty about partial disarmament is that each side maneuvers to keep the weapon that best suits its strategy and its temperament. The shopping lists never match—as the League of Nations ruefully discovered in the thirties. The only way out of the impasse is the bold way chosen in the Baruch Plan—and tragically rejected by the Russians—and that is to take the weapons out of the nations' hands and put them into international keeping. Beyond the local police forces and local militia needed for normal internal security, the world's arms should be in the hands of the world's permanent international police force, and this and nothing less should be the ultimate aim of all parleys on disarmament.

The idea may seem fantastic, utopian, impossible, unimaginable. But are push-button rockets any less so? What sort of a world shall we create if every tool, gadget or machine is powered to the ultimate degree, if all time sequences are altered and space itself is turned inside out while institutions and policies remain totally unchanged? If we can think no new thoughts under the shadow of atomic destruction, then there may not be much time left in which to think any thoughts at all.

At present, ultimate disarmament is not the aim of the negotiating Powers. They are maneuvering to keep the kind of arms which will make their own aims and interests secure. We have not passed beyond the age of private violence. Yet with each new lurch of the world to the brink of war, the number of voices raised to end this insanity and to support the institutions which alone give some hope of doing so, seems to increase and, more hopeful still, actual experiments in international policing have been launched. Nor is it ruled out that a permanent UN force may be created to act in the kind of emergencies that have arisen so constantly in the Middle East in recent years and can arise wherever the aftermath of empire leaves the area fluid and confused and open to all manner of local and external pressures. The world is caught in two minds—between the old mind of national interests and total sovereignty and a new mind fumbling toward concepts of peace under law. No one would be bold enough to forecast which way the decision will fall. But some things can be said with certainty about the forces which determine the choice.

IV

Perhaps a third of mankind lives in what are called "the uncommitted nations." Some of these nations are great and powerful. Most of them are small and new and—in a world where industry and science increase steadily the power of those who are already powerful and as steadily increase the gap between great and small—one might expect them to exercise little influence or direct effect upon the great issues of the day.

This is not so, however. The liberal principle of self-determination and the democratic principle of national equality have given the smaller Powers a voice they have never enjoyed before in human history and a fulcrum in the United Nations through which they can bring their influence to bear. There can be no doubt that the great Powers seek to maneuver this floating opinion of mankind over to their side in the public discussion of issues, and there is equally no doubt that a determined drive on the part of the uncommitted could secure modifications in world policies. In other words, the old African proverb does not entirely apply. We have the unusual spectacle of the bull elephants paying some attention to the grass. It is not there simply to be trampled on. It has a voice. There is, as it were, a "grass roots" opinion in international as well as in national society.

Since virtually all the members of the "uncommitted" community have emerged in the last twelve years from colonial status, their preoccupation with colonialism is perfectly understandable. But anti-colonialism can be only one strand in a balanced world outlook. It is a negative one, too. It describes very well what the uncommitted peoples do not want but makes no attempt to meet the more arduous problem of what they want in its place. If they want no more than national self-interest, and the right to do what they want, they plan for themselves exactly the kind of world that produces infallibly the enslavement of small peoples. If "want" and "will" are the only watchwords, Great Powers are much better at wanting and willing than their small neighbors and far more able to put their desires into effect.

This is the dilemma which the uncommitted nations have to face. They cannot propose limits to Great Power behavior which they do not accept for themselves. They cannot expect to be protected by a rule of law which they are ready to violate whenever their own interests are at stake. They cannot have anarchy at the lower levels of power and expect order at the top. So long, therefore, as the uncommitted nations propose international sanctions for everyone except themselves, they are in fact handing the governance of mankind back to the powerful and the ruthless, to the bull elephants in a jungle world.

(178)

There are, in fact, two kinds of neutrality. It is difficult to define which kind deserves the adjective "positive" or indeed what the adjective is supposed to mean. But the distinction is clear. There is a neutrality, a non-alignment between military blocs which seeks by all means to lessen the conflicts between them, to suggest solutions, to mediate difficulties, to press for orderly procedures and to aim steadily at an ultimate rule of law. I believe the Swedes have made a consistent effort to use their non-alignment for this purpose of strengthening, not weakening, the forces of reason and conciliation in world society. Nor do I think it possible to overestimate the influence a wider neutral bloc might exercise if it followed the same *truly positive* approach to world order. Then indeed the bull elephants would have to listen not simply to platitudes and slogans but to hard, shrewd, concrete comments on their manner of handling and mishandling human affairs. And I believe the pressure on them to act on such promptings would steadily increase.

But there is another non-alignment which regards neutrality as a sort of seesaw in which, by playing one bloc off against another—now swinging down with Communist support, now soaring up with Western backing—local plans, plots, and objectives can be secured. Yet what kind of security is to be found on a seesaw? Is this not precisely the posture of maximum instability? For a time, the balancing act may secure spectacular results but with every new crisis, the general atmosphere of tension grows more charged, the cost in frayed nerves and exhausted patience mounts, the invitation to outside intervention grows more irresistible. And what do the few local victories look like when the day of reckoning brings with it death, destruction, and probably the loss of independence as well? We have seen enough of the results of this type of neutrality in the Middle East to say that, whatever its title, it has nothing positive to contribute to the well-being of man.

Each new and uncommitted nation has, then, its choice of neutrality—the flaming, posturing, "positive" type or the patient, constructive neutrality which accepts the rule of law, for itself and others, supports and finances experiments in international supervision, and urges upon all Powers, great and small alike, the behavior which alone can ensure survival in the narrow planet they all have to share. As the strength of this type of non-alignment grows, so will the prospects for "a calm world and a long peace." May it be Ghana's, as this young nation steps out into the arena of world affairs.

V

But the great decisions are still made by the Great Powers. What can we hope from them? Perhaps the most appropriate summary of the modifications they need to make for human survival is to suggest that the Communist Powers need to abandon their picture of world order and the Western Powers need to acquire one.

It can be said with categorical certainty that no world order can ever be exclusively Communist and controlled from Moscow. There are no "objective" economic laws bringing this consummation about. Men are too various, too diverse, and too unconditioned for more than very general conclusions to be drawn about their behavior, and to these general conclusions there will always be the great, skyrocketing exception that changes destiny and transforms history and compels the drawing of quite new conclusions about the human drama. No one could have foreseen, no one could have objectively deduced the impact on the whole development of human history of two small peoples in the Eastern Mediterranean—the Greeks and the Jews. We do not know today what new destinies are already shaping in the womb of time. But we do know they will differ in character and impact as widely from our present expectations as does twentieth-century welfare capitalism from Marx's predicted growth of Inevitable Immiseration.

Besides, even if the impossibility of total Communism were not ruled out *a priori* by our knowledge of human history, we can already see after forty years that the picture will not stick. Titoism finished for all time the notion that, once a state became Communist, it would predictably remain a satellite of Moscow. Since then, the Chinese revolution has made it certain that no inevitable finger of destiny points to Moscow as the center of world Communism and the "Third Rome." Peking already plays an independent role. As its industrialization increases and its dependence on Soviet bounty lessens, this independence will increase, and no iron economic laws exist to ensure that Moscow and Peking will always want the same thing.

In a halting, hesitating way, Khrushchev has admitted from time to time that there may be more than one road to socialism. It is the first welcome sign of a return to the reality principle. If it could be expanded and developed into the admission that nations will take more than one road not only to Socialism but to the whole apparatus of modernization, there might be a reduction in Communist pressure in unstable areas, more readiness to let others make their own experiments, less worldwide conspiratorial activity to bring about a Communist millennium which is already a demonstrable impossibility.

Such changes in Communism's external activity have occurred. Until 1955, for example, Mr. Nehru was the "running dog of Western Imperialism." Then, overnight, he became a great nationalist leader of the uncommitted peoples. So far, such modifications have been purely tactical, while the grand strategy of total Communization remains. Yet if time reinforces the lesson that there are different roads to socialism, or for that matter, to capitalism, cooperativism, pluralism, and every and any other method of organizing the business of our daily bread, is it too much to hope that the Communists' strategy may change too, that the missionaries and the activists and the busy men from Agitprop may be called off and the world relieved of the extra dimension of

Communist mischief-making which now besets every problem it has to solve?

Perhaps it is too soon for the missionary phase to have passed. Yet each hour gained for peace in our mixed, experimental, unpredictable world means one more chance for the myth of a total and universal Communist world order to fade before the light of reality and common day.

If the Communists need to shed their vision of world order, the Western Powers need to gain one—not, I hasten to say, a comparably ideological and rigid picture but rather a sense of community and responsibility shared with all mankind. I do not believe they possess a consistent view today. The European Powers have sloughed off colonialism too recently to be fully alive to the realities of the new world they have helped to create. America is by tradition too prosperous, too fortunate, too protected to feel, naturally and urgently, the necessity of world policies or of a world strategy for peace. The result of this vacuum is that Western policy has tended to be a simple reaction to the various Communist dealings, a rushing to and fro, plugging up one hole as a new one bursts through, immersed in tactics, void of broad strategy and never quite catching up on one crisis before the next one looms and breaks.

To this disarray, there is only one answer—a broad, flexible policy for dealing with a world in which all nations are neighbors for good and ill and from which no state, however powerful, can cash out into prosperous isolation. If this fundamental fact of community is accepted, there can be little dispute over the principles of Western world policy because they are the principles already rooted in the foundations of its domestic life. Western societies base their freedom upon law and upon the abandonment of private violence. If they do so at home, they must do so abroad, and Western pressure should be ceaselessly and tirelessly at work not simply in the one-sided defense of national interests—which still occupies nine-tenths of diplomacy—but in search of the greatest of all national interests, survival through law.

Not even the warmest partisans of Western policy can maintain that in the postwar years an utterly uncompromising and undeviating search for supervised disarmament and the establishment of an international legal and policing system have been a first priority on the agenda of every Western foreign minister or secretary of state. The Communists were even able in the decade before the Hungarian disaster practically to monopolize the field of propaganda for disarmament in the misleading guise of the atomic ban.

The West cannot afford to repeat that apparent indifference. Every effort of diplomacy, every means of rallying world opinion, every instrument of publicity and public education should underline Western readiness to accept the basic institutions of a law-abiding world society and to negotiate for years, for decades if necessary, to bring them into force. Meanwhile, the intermediate stages of such a program—local police forces, the creation of areas of non-intervention, limited experiments in arms control—should be vigorously pressed.

This part of a Western program depends upon the agreement of others. Unilateral disarmament is not a prelude to world order. It is an invitation to world anarchy. The nations can give up ultimate self-defense only to a fully agreed supervised and policed alternative. But there is another broad area in which Western action depends solely upon its own decision.

Here too, the pointers of domestic society mark out the way. The original brutal industrialism which Marx foresaw as an instrument of deepening misery has been transformed by the humane and Christian traditions of the West. The transformation is still in process, and no one would claim that the plural economies of the West bear any resemblance yet to the ultimate millennium. But they have achieved a wider degree of social justice, they have created margins unknown before of well-being for everyone, they have set the machinery of industrial society to work for the mass of men as well as for the privileged few. And if one policy more than any other has been responsible for this, it is the principle that the wealth created by the collective efforts of so many men and women should in due measure be shared by all. This is the welfare principle which has transformed Western industrialization in the last century.

Today large areas of the world stand where Britain stood in the 1840's. The great economic transformations are beginning, the first brutal phase of capital accumulation is at hand. At the same time, the Atlantic nations in which the modern economic revolution started soonest and under fairest conditions have now reached a position of prosperity which makes them the affluent elite of a new world society. They draw that wealth not only from their own work but from the efforts of a whole interdependent world economy. The migrant Bantu laborer sends his ounce of gold to Fort Knox. But for most of humanity, the wealth trickles down more slowly than it ever did in Victorian England. The coolie in the rice paddies may earn $30 a year. The Atlantic worker brings home his $750 and more.

Under these conditions, if the fact of world community is accepted, there is only one conclusion to be drawn—that the wealthy Western peoples are challenged to repeat at the international level the acts of justice, vision, and generosity which enabled them to transform industrialism at home. The principle is the same. So, in appropriate form, is the practice, for it is simply to see that a tithe of the wealth created in the world is shared more evenly with all the world's workers. Put at a very minimum, this principle could command the transfer of one or two percent of the West's rising national income to the developing nations and this annual sum of $10 to $12 billion in development capital would provide the essential motive power to lift the emergent peoples through the first phase of capital accumulation and set them on the way to creating their own means of further growth.

The policy would do more than create the economic possibility of expansion. In this present worldwide phase of rapid modernization, it would mitigate the rigors of early industrialism and prevent the imposition of political disciplines too harsh for the survival of a liberal society.

I do not argue the West's clear self-interest in this vital, new, international extension of the principle of welfare. No doubt it is there, for who are more interested than the prosperous Western peoples in seeing the world economy grow and flourish? But I do not believe self-interest alone would ever have been sufficient to work the transformation from misery to welfare within the Western economy, and I doubt if national self-interest is enough to bring about the same revolution at the international level. My faith is that the shaping forces of social justice, humane concern, and Christian compassion, which Marx dismissed as worthless bourgeois windowdressing, represent on the contrary the essential expression of the free spirit. So long as compassion and personal responsibility are active in human souls, freedom can survive and act and reshape human institutions, however encrusted they may seem with human prejudice and human greed.

These forces conquered the citadels of self-interest and irresponsibility inside Western society. They must now work to enlarge our vision to include the whole family of man. I confess that it is to them, and not simply to the narrow dictates of interest, that I look for a better, richer future and for a peaceful home for all mankind.